8 KEYS TO ELIMINATING PASSIVE-AGGRESSIVENESS

8 Keys to Mental Health Series

Babette Rothschild, Series Editor

The 8 Keys series of books provides consumers with brief, inexpensive, and high-quality self-help books on a variety of topics in mental health. Each volume is written by an expert in the field, someone who is capable of presenting evidence-based information in a concise and clear way. These books stand out by offering consumers cutting-edge, relevant theory in easily digestible portions, written in an accessible style. The tone is respectful of the reader and the messages are immediately applicable. Filled with exercises and practical strategies, these books empower readers to help themselves.

8 KEYS TO ELIMINATING PASSIVE-AGGRESSIVENESS

STRATEGIES FOR TRANSFORMING YOUR RELATIONSHIPS FOR GREATER AUTHENTICITY AND JOY

ANDREA BRANDT

FOREWORD BY BABETTE ROTHSCHILD

W. W. Norton & Company
New York · London

For information about permission to reproduce selections
from this book, write to Permissions, W. W. Norton & Company, Inc.,
500 Fifth Avenue, New York, NY 10110

For information about special discounts for bulk purchases, please contact
W. W. Norton Special Sales at specialsales@wwnorton.com or 800-233-4830

Manufacturing by RR Donnelley, Harrisonburg
Production manager: Leeann Graham

Library of Congress Cataloging-in-Publication Data
Brandt, Andrea.
8 keys to eliminating passive-aggressiveness / Andrea Brandt ;
foreword by Babette Rothschild. — First edition.
pages cm — (8 keys to mental health series)
Includes bibliographical references and index.
ISBN 978-0-393-70846-2 (pbk.)
1. Passive-aggressive personality. 2. Anger. 3. Interpersonal communication.
I. Title. II. Title: Eight keys to eliminating passive-aggressiveness.
RC569.5.P37B73 2013
616.85'81—dc23
2013027762

ISBN: 978-0-393-70846-2 (pbk.)

W. W. Norton & Company, Inc.
500 Fifth Avenue, New York, N.Y. 10110
www.wwnorton.com

W. W. Norton & Company Ltd.
Castle House, 75/76 Wells Street, London W1T 3QT

1 2 3 4 5 6 7 8 9 0

To my clients, past and present, who have inspired me with their courage, growth, and transformation.

To my husband, JP—your love, encouragement, and support make all things possible.

Contents

Acknowledgments

A special thanks to the following people, for the important role they have played in the development of this book. To each, I am very grateful.

Babette Rothschild, for recognizing my work in the field of anger and calling on me to participate in her groundbreaking series. Without her, this book wouldn't have happened.

Brookes Nohlgren, my invaluable partner on this project, who really gets me and is able to translate my stories, notes, observations, anecdotes, and knowledge into a comprehensive tool for transformation and change.

Deborah Malmud, director of Norton Professional Books, for her guidance and support.

Fay Hove, for her dedication and loyalty, and whose feedback and good nature make for a great working relationship.

Colleagues and friends—who often overlap—for being instrumental in my personal, professional, and intellectual growth. Their support, insight, and enthusiasm continually propel me forward.

Curt Batiste, for his brilliance and openness, and for challenging me to broaden my perspective and for lowering my anxiety when I needed it most.

Ron Poze, where it all began!

Pat Ogden, for teaching me how the body-mind connection could transform my work and encouraging me to take the risk.

Never least, my family, without whom I wouldn't have a personal understanding of passive-aggressiveness.

Foreword

Babette Rothschild, Series Editor

We tend to use the term *passive-aggressive* quite liberally to describe behavior that we find annoying in others. "Oh, he is being
so passive-aggressive!" More accurately, passive-aggressiveness describes a variety of behaviors that range from the merely meekly
non-assertive to the outright hostile. For little understood reasons,
of all human traits and behaviors, passive-aggressiveness is, for
most of us, one of the most difficult to deal with. We are exposed
to some degree of passive-aggressiveness on a daily basis. It perme-
ates all types and levels of relationships as well as communication
in both personal and professional settings. Most of us are familiar
with it, whether it is ingrained in our own behavior or a feature of
the behavior of those around us. In some families it can be a tradi-
tion, in some organizations it can be protocol, and in some settings, it can even be the norm rather than the exception, wreaking
havoc on the most basic of interactions and relationships. It can
become an ingrained behavioral style in someone, not because of
an intention to be difficult or evasive, but because that is exactly
how many people learn they can (and in some cases, *should*) get
their needs met. Passive-aggressiveness is truly a difficult and
complex mechanism.

Fortunately, Andrea Brandt is up to the task of tackling such a
challenging issue. I first approached her to write a book for the 8
Keys to Mental Health Series because I knew her fine reputation as
a specialist in anger management. She is a sought-after expert and

has appeared on numerous talk shows. She has decades of experience working with and teaching people to better acknowledge and more effectively express their anger. Rather than judging passive-aggressive people, she has identified that passive-aggressiveness is a cultural dilemma that grows from society's taboos against anger itself. Because anger is not widely accepted within our friend networks, families, and professional groups, indirect communication becomes the more familiar strategy for many people.

While many will malign those who use passive-aggressiveness as their communicative mode of choice, Brandt takes a compassionate view of the dilemma of the passive-aggressive person, puts her arm around their shoulder, and shows them ways they can more effectively say what they think and get what they need. First Brandt deftly identifies and defines the characteristics of passive-aggressiveness using clear examples that readers will find familiar. Then she offers 8 keys for changing the pattern into one of effective communication and assertiveness. Through engaging, illustrative case examples and exercises that teach insight and useful skills, you will learn how to use clear communication and effective assertiveness to replace the habit of passive-aggressiveness. Friends, loved ones, and colleagues of passive-aggressive individuals will also be helped to better manage and respond in frustrating and aggravating situations. Throughout the book, Brandt connects the most relevant dots—body/mind, mindfulness, boundaries, emotions, and thoughts—to present a truly holistic approach to changing passive-aggressive patterns. With every page I found myself feeling more compassion and kindness toward my own patterns of passive-aggressiveness and the passive-aggressiveness I encounter from others, while gaining a better supply of tools for dealing with those difficult encounters.

Readers will find 8 *Keys to Eliminating Passive-Aggressiveness* engaging, accessible, enlightening, and comforting. It is written to those who are prone to this behavior, and will help them as well as those in their sphere. It is a welcome addition to the 8 Keys to Mental Health Series, with a writing style that is immensely accessible and inviting. I felt cared for, understood, relevantly informed, and helped. I believe you will feel the same!

Understanding Passive-Aggressiveness and How It's Harming You

Sarah drove home from work thinking excitedly about the weekend she and her husband, Tom, had planned. They were going to drive up to the mountains to spend a leisurely and hopefully romantic couple of days. Exhausted from working overtime on a deadline the previous few weeks, Sarah was really looking forward to getting away with Tom.

When she walked into the house, she found a note from Tom that read, "At Jim's. Back later." Sarah started packing and waited for Tom to get home. As the hours passed, Sarah became more and more angry. They had talked about leaving before 8 p.m. so they could wake up Saturday at the resort and have the full weekend ahead of them.

Finally, around 11 p.m., Tom strolled in as if nothing were going on. At the beginning of their marriage, Sarah would have confronted him in a situation like this, but she had learned that if she got angry he would just walk away. She reminded him as calmly as she could about their plans. He simply shrugged his shoulders. "Something important came up," he said. "We can leave in the morning, if you really have your heart set on the trip."

To Sarah, his words were like a slap in the face. She could hear herself using the same explanation when business kept her away from home, and she wondered if Tom was needling her. She swallowed her anger and her hurt. "Well, I don't want *to interfere, if you have something so important to do," she said. "If you need time to take care of it, I suppose we can cancel our plans."*

Now let's look at Tom's side of the story.

Tom was home earlier than Sarah—wasn't that always the way? Her job was much more important than his, and she made significantly more money. Tom insisted that he wasn't upset by that difference, but it got to him that Sarah was never home. For the last five or six weeks he'd hardly seen her, and now, the first weekend she'd had any time for him, she wanted to run off to some fancy resort that she'd have to pay for. Tom really didn't want to go, but he hated to say no to her. It was her money, after all.

He looked around for something to do while he was waiting for her to come home and saw some tools he should return to his neighbor, Jim. He wrote her a short note and left. Jim offered him a beer. They got to talking, and then there was a basketball game on TV and Tom lost track of time.

When he got home, he saw that it was late, and Sarah looked angry—just like his mother. He didn't see why it was such a big deal. She was gone a lot of evenings. So they would save the money for one night's lodging. Why was she upset?

On the surface, both Sarah and Tom sound so civil and reasonable, yet it's clear that a lot of hostility has been generated. Tom's behavior bears the markers of passive-aggressiveness:

- He hides his anger about the time Sarah's job takes away from their life together; he probably doesn't even know he's angry.
- He doesn't tell Sarah how he feels about the resort plans; he doesn't want to say no.
- Perhaps without intending to, he manages to sabotage the plan by leaving the house for the evening.
- He sees that Sarah's upset, but he can't see why.

Sarah, in turn, makes her own contribution to their impasse. She knows she's angry, but she's careful not to show it. And when

Tom seems unconcerned about his lateness, she isn't sure what's going on inside his head. Instead of revealing her hurt feelings, she picks up a passive-aggressive style: "Never mind," she says, "we don't need to go at all."

The truth is that everyone occasionally responds in a passive-aggressive way. We say yes when we want to say no. Because anger is such a shunned emotion in our culture, we're all at something of a loss when we feel it stirring inside us. We'll do almost anything rather than show how we feel—angry—and risk creating conflict. What we don't understand or acknowledge is that anger doesn't go away if we ignore it. It is an energy that demands to be expressed. Passive-aggressive behavior is a means for us to show our anger in a subversive, seemingly consequence-free way. The person we're dealing with may well feel a jab from our unspoken hostility, but *our* words and actions are unimpeachable. We believe in our innocence, that we have done nothing wrong.

What is an occasional slip of indirect communication for many people, however, is a full-fledged life strategy for some. These men and women—and those who live and work with them—are the audience this book hopes to address. Whether you suffer from passive-aggression yourself or are involved in a relationship with someone who does, my goal is to help you understand this challenging behavior pattern and bring an end to its reign over your life. Having an awareness of how it is in play is half the battle of making a better choice.

In this introduction, we'll explore passive-aggression in more detail and look at its sources. Then I'll offer eight keys to help those of you with passive-aggressive tendencies to find new ways to relate to your anger and to express your needs to others more directly. Within each key, I'll also offer reliable strategies for the *partners* (which in this book means spouse or romantic partner, friend, co-worker, boss, employee, parent, adult child, or sibling—any substantial relationship) who inadvertently find themselves caught up in a passive-aggressive tango. These methods can help both of you to disengage from the cycle and to start taking effective steps to eliminate passive-aggressiveness from your life.

To a large degree, knowledge is power, but this book will also provide concrete exercises you can use to change your approach to anger and the devastating effect it can have on your relationships, no matter which role you play in the passive-aggressive encounter. Let's get started.

What Is Your Personality Pattern?

Roberta and Joyce have an apartment together. They buy groceries out of a shared household purse and save money by shopping once a week at a big-box store. A half gallon of milk there is cheaper than two quarts at the local supermarket.

When Joyce goes to add milk to her cereal one morning, however, there's just a tablespoon or two left in the bottom of the carton. "What happened to the milk?" she asks Roberta, who is getting ready to walk out the door on her way to work.

"Are we out?" Roberta says. "You know, my friend Jack made himself hot cocoa last night. He must have taken the last of it. Sorry."

Depending on her personality patterns, here are four possible ways Joyce might respond.

A. "Well, you should try thinking—if you can figure out how," Joyce replies, hurling the nearly empty carton at Roberta. Some of the milk splashes onto her skirt. "Is Jack contributing to our household budget now? I hope he enjoyed *my* milk."
B. "That's okay," Joyce says. "I'll get coffee on the way to work." Coffee, of course, will cost money, and she can never resist the scones at Starbucks. But she doesn't want Roberta to be upset. "Have a good day," she says.
C. Joyce takes a deep breath. "We have to rethink our shopping list, I guess, or maybe shop at the local market when we see supplies running low ahead of schedule. Let's talk it over tonight."

D. "Oh, that's okay," Joyce says softly. "I'll just find something else for breakfast." She's remembering a container of Roberta's favorite yogurt, the last on the shelf.

Which response most closely fits what you would do in a similar situation? *Be honest.* This is a book about passive-aggression, but only one of the responses matches that behavior pattern. If you have trouble with passive-aggression yourself, or you are reading this book because someone in your life does, you will probably recognize that choice. But let's see what each response indicates.

A is for an aggressive personality. Aggression is usually impulsive, but the intention is to hurt. There's minor physical violence in the thrown milk carton, but the more troublesome violence is emotional—a gratuitous insult and some innuendo about Roberta's male friend. Anger is highly visible here.

B is a passive personality. People who respond passively don't express their needs or protect their rights, often because their low self-esteem makes them feel unworthy compared to almost everyone in their lives. We don't see anger here, but it's hard to imagine that someone will live this way for long without developing a large pool of hidden anger.

C is an assertive personality. That deep breath says a lot. Joyce feels her anger rising, and she takes the time to examine it before she responds. The problem, she sees, is an inadequate supply of milk. Roberta's friend just happened to be the one who got the last portion. Their needs have collided, and it's time for a discussion—a positive and responsible approach to solving the issue.

D is a classic passive-aggressive personality. No anger is visible here. When Roberta looks for her yogurt this evening, Joyce will sweetly reply that she had to have *some-*

thing for breakfast, and that was all she could find. How can Roberta be angry? In a way, Joyce just took what she was owed. But Roberta may feel the sting, too, particularly if she and Joyce have known each other for a while.

What Is Passive-Aggression?

Passive-aggressiveness, also called passive-aggression, is a way to express angry feelings in a seemingly nonhostile way. Since no definition can clarify the meaning as vividly as examples, let's explore a few scenarios that demonstrate escalating levels of passive-aggression.

> *Lucy hates to get up in the morning. Her mother calls and calls to wake her up, but she lingers under the covers, pretending not to hear. Actually, Lucy has a pretty good idea of when her mother will come pounding up the stairs to knock on her door. She makes sure she's on her feet and headed for the bathroom by that time.*

Sounds simple enough, right? A variation of this is something we all probably did more than a few times during childhood. Or maybe we turned the television off and started our homework, but not when we were asked the first time. By complying, but with a delay, we created anger in our parent. Lucy's mother, as no doubt the rest of our mothers did, started her morning irritated at our behavior.

Let's see what happens when passive-aggression gets a bit worse.

> *To try to end this little power struggle, Lucy's mother takes a new tack in dealing with Lucy. She tells Lucy that, from here on out, she's only going to call her once. If Lucy doesn't get up when her mother calls, then she'll have to get herself to school, which means walking or waiting for the bus. The next morning, Lucy gets up at the first call, but she takes her time in the family's only bathroom, brushing her teeth and washing her*

face. When she opens the door, the whole family is gathered outside, their schedules upset because they couldn't use the bathroom themselves. "I was just trying to do what you asked," Lucy yawns. "I guess I'm just a little slow when I'm still half asleep."

To her family, Lucy's foot-dragging may seem intentional, but Lucy herself may not understand her motivation or mean the harm. After all, she was only following orders, and she has a ready explanation. Her family members are left to deal with their annoyance. We see in this scenario the roots of a passive-aggressive approach to life.

Let's check in on Lucy a couple of years down the road.

When the phone rings, Lucy sees that the call is from her father's partner. Instead of letting it go to the answering machine, she picks it up and offers to take a message. Her dad's partner says that, rather than meeting at work in the morning, her father should go directly to the airport for a flight to an important business meeting. Lucy picks up a pencil and makes a note. She even asks for the time of the flight. Then she tosses the note toward the small kitchen desk where her dad keeps his briefcase, and she goes to watch TV.

While the family is eating dinner that evening, Lucy's dad gets a call on his cell phone and hangs up angry. "When were you going to tell me about the flight change, Lucy?"

Lucy looks up. "Flight change? Oh, yeah, your partner called."

Her father takes a deep breath. "And he says you took a message."

"Sure," she says, walking to his desk. "It's right here." She bends over. "Oops, it must have fallen on the floor when you put your briefcase down. I'm sorry." She hands him the carefully written note.

Was Lucy simply careless? Or was she reacting to her father's refusal to let her go to a party with some older friends on Saturday night? Her family can't say, and Lucy may not know herself. She would have made sure he saw the note before bedtime, right? This tactic of inaction is passive-aggressive nonetheless.

The next example involves action.

> *Lucy's in college now. Not the out-of-state college she wanted to attend, the one with the cool campus and the great football team; her parents said the tuition was way above their means to pay. Instead she's at a college her parents said they could "manage somehow" (and that was before her mother was laid off), a couple of hours along the freeway from home. They have given her a credit card to use for school expenses, so she loads it to the max buying a new laptop computer. She tells her parents that her professors "are practically requiring everyone to have a laptop," even though she has a lot of nonacademic uses in mind. She may believe that the credit card was their olive branch for sending her to a second-string school.*

By now, Lucy is totally in the grip of passive-aggression. Although her parents might see this as vengeful action, Lucy probably believes that she's entitled to what she's taken. Her passive-aggression has moved along to other relationships.

> *Lucy's roommate, Penny, is very pretty, and she looks particularly good in a pale peach sweater. Lucy "borrows" it and somehow spills red wine on it. She tosses it in the bottom of her own closet, where it lies for a few days until her roommate starts looking for it to attend a fraternity mixer. "Oh my gosh," Lucy says, "I didn't want you to see it until I had a chance to get it to the cleaners. I'm so sorry."*

Let's take a look at what Lucy's life tells us about passive-aggression.

In its mildest form, passive-aggressive behavior is something we can all probably recognize in ourselves. We've all said yes, only to reveal the truth of our feelings by not following through.

At the mall, for example, we take a form to make a charitable donation and then throw it on the floor of the car. We agree to prepare something for a school event, but somehow the task falls to the bottom of the to-do list. We say we'll do a chore but become engrossed in a more desirable activity and simply forget.

What's missing in this type of scenario—at least in most cases—is the key component in passive-aggression: anger. Every time her mother called to wake her up, Lucy got a little more annoyed, but she stayed cool on the outside, while her mother raised her voice. A kindred spirit is the office worker who puts a disagreeable task from a disagreeable boss at the bottom of the in-basket. Or the husband who is always forgetting his wife's grocery list when he goes out to the store.

Lucy's hostility was more evident—but not overt—when she held the bathroom hostage. At this stage in passive-aggression, people may manage to mess up the outcome, even while making every apparent effort to do what they're told. Say that Jack does the dishes, but he manages to break two glasses in the process. "I'm just kind of clumsy," he explains.

Crimes of omission are another aspect of passive-aggressiveness. Lucy knew the message for her father was important. Whether or not she actually threw it on the floor, she made no effort to call it to her dad's attention. Passive-aggressiveness often involves forgetting to deliver information or take steps because you're angry at someone, when you know that person will get hurt.

Passive-aggression can include acts of revenge, like Lucy's credit card overruns, but note that she felt she was entitled to the laptop. She didn't see the purchase as a deliberate attempt to hit her parents where it would hurt.

How, you might ask, do people get this way?

Well, first of all, as a psychologist who's worked with thousands of patients, I can honestly say there is no such thing as a bad seed. I repeat: *There is no such thing as a bad seed, a bad child, a bad person.* Behaving passive-aggressively doesn't make you bad, nor does the anger that lies beneath your behavior. However, I deliberately chose a child/adolescent to provide my examples of passive-aggression, because the roots of passive-aggression usually lie in our formative years.

And I want to add that while the behavior I've described here is definitely unacceptable, I have as much empathy for Lucy as I have for her confused and angry parents and all the other people Lucy will injure until she understands her problematic behavior. Passive-aggression is a problem for everyone in its circle, the perpetrators as well as their various partners. This book is designed to help both sides escape from the often devastating effects of this misguided life strategy.

Let's look at the origins of passive-aggression so that we can develop an understanding of people like Lucy who are caught in its web.

Where Does It Begin?

Passive-aggression is a coping mechanism people use when they perceive themselves to be powerless or when they fear that using their power will lead to bad outcomes—to conflict or loss of company. Not surprisingly, then, the root behaviors of passive-aggression are found in childhood, when all of us are, to varying degrees, powerless to control many facets of our lives.

We are dependent on our parents or guardians for the basics of food, shelter, and clothing. We're required by law to attend school, where our days are more or less regimented by the instructional agenda. Ideally, children find that parents or guardians meet their emotional as well as physical needs. Craving stability, nurturance, and protection, they grow up with a sense of belonging to a family; they learn to trust; they share affection. Between home and school, they develop competence and the self-confidence that goes with it. By being cared for, they learn to care about significant others in their lives.

This is not the universal experience, however, and it may not even represent a majority. Some relationships within the family can lead directly to passive-aggression, while others promote it. The following are some of the ways it can start.

Aggression + Passiveness = Passive-Aggression

If one parent is dominant and the other is subservient, children will almost inevitably develop some passive-aggressive tendencies. They may have an excellent role model in the subservient parent, who may be dealing with the dominant partner through passive-aggression. "We won't tell your father," the passive-aggressive partner says, spending money for childhood treats behind Dad's back. The child learns that powerful or volatile people can't be approached directly, but it's okay to lie to them or keep secrets to get what you want.

Almost inevitably, feelings of anger and hostility toward the dominant parent will arise, and children may become engaged in the subservient parent's dishonest communication and even acts of sabotage. Again, for the child with passive-aggression, the anger toward and the desire for revenge against the dominant/domineering parent may become a hidden or unconscious pattern for dealing with authority figures throughout life.

Other early influences—older siblings, relatives, and friends—may also provide role models for passive-aggressive behavior. A social culture of hiding negative feelings also contributes.

Withheld Acceptance

One of the major roles of parents is to establish standards for their children that promote their success in life and shape their perspectives and behaviors in ways that will help them deal with the world as adults. Unrealistic standards, however, can lead children to develop passive-aggression as a way to evade the burden of expectations they don't think they can meet—and the blame for failure.

The distinction here is between good behavior and a good child. Children need to know that their parents love them, even if they get a C instead of an A in school, even if they get their clothes dirty playing, even if they break a window throwing a base-ball, even if they get in a fight with the kid down the street.

Faced with unreasonably rigid parents, children will quickly learn that they must always appear to be charming, cooperative, and agreeable. The pressure of maintaining this "false self" will create a great deal of anxiety and direct the child to passive-aggressive channels for dealing with her or his own needs.

Low Self-Esteem

In recent years, we've come to recognize the pernicious and pervasive problems that a person's low self-esteem can bring—whether or not there is any supporting evidence for the person's self-evaluation. Often, there is no relationship at all between an objective view of people's intelligence and abilities and their own assessment. Even those who don't live in Garrison Keillor's Lake Wobegon—where "all the children are above average"—should learn as children that they nevertheless have value and gifts that they bring to others in their social circle.

If this lesson never occurs, they may grow into adults who al-ways feel like the "second banana" in their relationships, who see themselves as inherently unworthy of having their needs met by asking for what they want. Passive-aggression is a strategy they may come to rely on more and more, particularly if they find it effec-tive, not only for getting what they want, but also for feeling the sense of power they thought would always elude them.

Fear of Feelings

As a society, we've become obsessed with happiness. The "happy days" theme of one generation goes with the ubiquitous happy face of another. Once I asked a young Indian graduate student whether he was experiencing culture shock. What bothered him most, he said, was that when people asked, "How are you?" they didn't re-ally want to know. "Great" was the expected answer—even "Okay" raised an eyebrow.

All of our more uncomfortable emotions—such as loneliness, anger, sadness, anxiety, fear—are supposed to be tucked in a cupboard somewhere, out of sight. We don't show them, and we don't expect to see them from others. Too many times, in hiding them, we lose sight of them ourselves. *Of course,* we tell ourselves, *we're happy.*

Passive-aggression is a mask we can wear to cover all of our unacceptable emotions. If we do it well enough, we may even forget what's there.

Fear of Conflict and Fear of Loss

People are ill at ease with conflict—even when it originates in rational and well-considered differences of opinion and is expressed quite civilly. The carryover in our own lives is that we will go a long way to ignore or disguise the differences we have with significant others.

Underlying the fear of conflict in these cases is a fear that somehow the conflict will lead to separation. We don't express our feelings because we leap to the conclusion that any difference of opinion will lead to a quarrel, and that any quarrel will threaten the relationship. It's easier to bite our tongue—think of the pain that metaphor entails—than take that risk. So we "keep our piece"—and that's the correct spelling, by the way; what we keep has little or nothing to do with *peace*, which is undermined in the long run when people don't share their thoughts and feelings with each other.

Childhood Abuse

Some people who are abused as children—assaulted physically, psychologically, or sexually—respond in kind. They grow into aggressive youth and criminally violent adults. Others plunge into a passive life of victimhood, finding situations as adults where they can replay the violence they experienced as children, always hoping for a different outcome. The woman who goes from one abusive partner to another is an example of this option. An abusive relationship is the only kind of relationship she knows.

Passive-aggression offers a less direct and seemingly safer pathway. Fearing—with reason—the angry and violent responses that
might greet any of their demands, children learn to manipulate
others to get their needs met. Most of all, they learn that authority
figures have a monopoly on the *display* of anger. Recognizing that
they have virtually no power over the hostile adults in their environment, they suppress their aggressive feelings. By a sort of psychological alchemy, those repressed feelings create a toxic brew
of resentment, anger, and revenge. All of this can be summed up
in the childish threat: "Just wait until I'm big and you're little."

Once rewarded as a childhood strategy, this way of dealing
with others is likely to become ingrained, carrying over into adult
relationships with partners, friends, neighbors, bosses, and colleagues. It becomes a way of dealing with all of life and especially
with others perceived to be authority figures, even when they pose
no threat.

Hidden Anger

Because expressions of anger have become widely unacceptable in
our society, children learn at an early age to repress anger or at the
very least to avoid displaying it openly—so successfully that they
may no longer recognize that they *are* angry.

In many respects, hidden anger is the underlying theme in all
the situations we've discussed. It's easy to see how abused children
will become angry, but so will children whose lives are organized
by a domineering or overly demanding parent, children who never
seem to please, who feel chronically less competent than others, or
whose parents are always too busy to give them the attention they
need. When we feel fear of conflict, what we're really feeling is a
fear that conflict will result in anger.

Hidden anger is so crucial to passive-aggression that we'll discuss it at length in Key 1. What I want to establish here is that
we've been uncovering a trail, looking at the origins of passive-
aggression and following it forward. Now we've reached the pot of
gold: Hidden anger is the thread that links various expressions of

passive-aggression, and it's also the key to breaking the habit and turning to a life where you are able to express your feelings and your needs calmly and effectively.

Advice for Partners

So far, I've focused on the people who display passive-aggressive behavior, but some of the emotional issues we're talking about here can be equally troubling for the partners who are trying to work out relationships with them.

Most of us come into adulthood trailing bad habits from our childhood years. Passive-aggression can be a hard game to play as a partner, even for the most emotionally healthy and stable individual. In many cases, however, partners have life experiences and behavioral strategies that complicate matters or make them worse. Their own personal histories and emotional choices make them enablers.

If you were raised in a family where one parent used passive-aggression, you may find it difficult to recognize that what's happening to you is not "normal." If you always worked overtime to please your parents, then you may spend a lot of time doing the same—without success—in your current relationship. Burdened with low self-esteem, you may feel that this is the best you can get—or worse yet, that it's what you deserve.

You may hesitate to challenge a partner's passive-aggressive behavior for fear of opening the door to conflict. In the meantime, however, you're building your own bulwark of hidden anger, and before long, your relationship could be deadlocked. That's what happened to Sarah and Tom.

How This Book Can Help

One of the key signs that you and your partner are involved in a relationship plagued by passive-aggression is that you find yourselves in a frustrating, lockstep cycle. You're both unhappy, you're both angry, but you don't know how to break this dysfunctional routine. *8 Keys to Eliminating Passive-Aggressiveness* aims to help you identify your problem, understand how you got into this situation, and start engaging in behaviors that will help you express your feelings and reach out to embrace each other with the love you both are seeking. Anecdotes throughout the book—composites of clients and other people I've known—will bring to life ways in which passive-aggressiveness can play out in relationships, while exercises will help you identify problem areas and facilitate change in your own life.

Key 1: Recognize Your Hidden Anger

Whether you're angry isn't the question—like the rest of us who belong to the human race, you are—and hiding this normal emotion isn't the answer. Anger is a great gift from your emotional self, and taking the time to listen to its message can change your life, whether you are in the grips of passive-aggression yourself or responding to a partner who is.

Key 2: Reconnect Your Emotions to Your Thoughts

People who suffer from passive-aggressive behavior are often telling people what they think instead of expressing how they feel. Partners may end up in confusion about how they feel in response. Whichever person you are, you will benefit from getting in touch with your authentic emotions. But before you can do that, you must sort through the unconscious beliefs that are running your life and directing you along the pathway of passive-aggression. Only then can your true emotions be revealed.

Key 3: Listen to Your Body

To help you get in touch with your authentic emotions, we turn to your body. Your body has a wealth of emotional information, and it never lies. You just need to start listening to it for its messages. Physical sensations are the body's primary language. Mindfulness—a strategy for attending to your sensations and emotions—can help you uncover your feelings and begin to act on them so that you gain power over your life.

Key 4: Set Healthy Boundaries

Beset by their own passive-aggression, people with this life strategy often have weak emotional boundaries, which are essential to our identity. Their partners also need to find ways to maintain their own stability and safety in the relationship. This discussion of boundaries will help restore the much needed sense of self and respect for others that both participants in every healthy relationship require.

Key 5: Communicate Assertively

Passive-aggression is all indirection, and when you don't ask for what you need, the odds of getting it are greatly reduced. You and your partner can learn to overcome the barrier you assembled long ago and begin to engage each other honestly. The result is greater happiness and intimacy.

Key 6: Reframe Conflict

Like anger, conflict has an undeservedly bad reputation. Acknowledging our differences and resolving them in honest but compassionate conflict is a way to increase the closeness of our relationships and ensure that the pools of unexpressed anger remain empty. It may be the only way to enable our relationships to grow stronger.

Key 7: Interact Using Mindfulness

Whether intentionally or not, those who engage in passive-aggression inflict a lot of damage on their partners. Taking responsibility for that hurt and learning to be mindful of your own feelings and those of your partner during interactions can bring new sensitivity, empathy, and consciously nurturing actions to your relationship.

Key 8: Disable the Enabler

In reality, passive-aggression is a tango between the person who adopts this strategy and the partner who chooses to accept it. In fact, partners are often in need of healing for childhood wounds that make their relationships more precarious. With this key, you will learn to replace accommodation with a healthy expression of negative feelings.

Turning these keys into productive change in your personal approach to life will take dedication and effort. Nothing worthwhile is easily achieved. Those who rely on passive-aggression—and often their partners—have to erase stubborn habits rooted in their neural pathways and engraved in their personality.

Those of you who are locked in a pattern of passive-aggressive behavior know better than anyone—even those who are closest to you—how much you suffer as a result. What a joy it would be to stand up for yourself, express your true feelings, and ask for what you need to make your life more fulfilling! That joy can be yours.

Others of you are committed to relationships with people whose behavior you often find confusing and frustrating. If you're staying with them, there's a connection between you that's worth cultivating. Passive-aggression is an obstacle standing in the way of your further intimacy. But people *can* change—if they want to do so. Together, you can disassemble passive-aggressiveness and pack it away in your past.

8 KEYS TO ELIMINATING PASSIVE-AGGRESSIVENESS

RECOGNIZE YOUR HIDDEN ANGER

S*helly couldn't understand what was happening. "Every-body is mad at me, and I don't know why," she thought. "It's like they all got together and decided to form a 'Dump on Shelly' party." The worst of it was at home. It seemed to Shelly that Peter, her husband, was exploding all the time at the least little thing she said.*

For instance, one day Peter said, "My boss gave me tickets to the Bears game on Sunday. I don't suppose you would want to go."

"Sure," Shelly said, "why not?"

"Really?" Peter said. "I thought you didn't like football."

"Well, I don't much, but you have tickets."

"Then why did you say 'Sure'?" Peter said, his voice rising. "You're always saying yes, and then you find some reason to back out. Will you really go this time?"

"Well, sure," Shelly said, "unless it's too cold. We can't sit outside in the cold."

"Shelly, it's November in Chicago. It's going to be cold," Peter said, shouting now. "Forget it." And he stormed out of the room.

Some readers are probably scratching their heads, wondering why Peter got so upset about this conversation. Others will be nodding their heads in understanding. Anger plays a central role in passive-aggressive behavior. For those who typically behave in this style—saying yes, for example, when they really mean no—the anger is deeply hidden. In childhood, they learned that displaying anger was a bad thing. In Shelly's case, her parents were authoritarian. What they wanted was agreement and compliance, and Shelly had learned her lesson well. For partners, passive-aggressive behavior can be exasperating. Like Peter, they know that apparent consent may be meaningless. It is, after all, November in Chicago.

Let's see how passive-aggressive behavior touches other areas of Shelly's life.

> Another person who always seemed to be angry with her these days was Marianne, the owner of the small retail shop where Shelly worked five days a week. Marianne was unreasonably critical of her work, Shelly felt. Just the other day, Marianne had called to her from the dressing room area, embarrassing Shelly while she was talking with a customer.
>
> The store had only three dressing rooms, and two of them had been piled high with discarded clothing, some still on hooks and hangers, others slipping off benches onto the floor.
>
> "I'm with a customer," Shelly had said as she approached Marianne.
>
> "And where is the customer going to try on the clothes you help her select?" Marianne asked, arms folded across her chest.
>
> Shelly pointed to the empty dressing room. "In here," she said. "I always keep one tidy."
>
> "And what do you suppose customers think about all the unwanted clothes in the other rooms? Didn't I ask you to rehang clothes just an hour ago?"
>
> "The customer . . ." Shelly said.
>
> "I'll take care of her," Marianne said. "You clean up the mess you've made."
>
> Shelly felt deeply ashamed as she turned to her task.

Passive-aggressive behavior may also become characteristic of relationships with others, especially authority figures like bosses. It's possible that the cluttered dressing rooms are a sign that Shelly is overworked, but that is a problem she needs to resolve with her employer. It's also possible that Shelly prefers to work with customers and tends to put other sales chores on the back burner until she has nothing else to do. She may be hearing the echo of her mother's voice in Marianne's orders to "clean up the mess you've made." Her feelings of shame underscore the childhood roots of her anger.

Expressions of anger are widely unacceptable in our society, and so most of us learn as children that we have to keep our anger "under control" at whatever cost. We are encouraged to suppress how we feel for the sake of keeping the peace with others. We associate this emotion with a loss of control, violence, guilt, and so on. We may even be told, "Don't *be* angry!"—as if the feeling itself were wrong. In time, if we have suppressed it enough, we may not even recognize when we're feeling anger because we're hiding it behind other, more acceptable emotions and rationales. Most of us reach adulthood either anger-phobic or afraid of confrontation. We simply don't know how to deal with anger. And it's certainly an uncomfortable feeling to experience in our bodies.

This is especially true for people who have developed passive-aggressive strategies for dealing with life. Anger—hidden, suppressed anger—is at the core of their behavior pattern. People who are long-term partners in a passive-aggressive relationship often have this trait, too. In a partnership where neither side knows how to express anger, real communication quickly comes to a standstill.

So what's the alternative? Instead of running away from our anger or "putting a lid on it," we need to stay with our angry feelings long enough to understand what they're trying to tell us. For many of us, this means recognizing that we are angry and then looking for the cause, a topic we will take up in other keys. Key 1 is devoted to learning to accept anger as a potential contributor to our well-being and identifying the sensations and feelings that tell us we are angry. First, we're going to explore the possibility that anger is a good emotion. Yes, you read that correctly. A *good, necessary emotion.*

Exercise: Tuning in to Hidden Anger

1. Find a quiet place where you can be uninterrupted for about 15 minutes, a place where you feel relaxed and safe.
2. Sit comfortably, keeping your torso upright, your arms and legs uncrossed, and your feet flat on the floor. After a minute, close your eyes and take a few deep breaths. Breathe in to the count of one, two, three . . . then out for one, two, three. Inhale and exhale again, repeating until you feel calm and your mind is clear of outside concerns.
3. Notice sensations and feelings first. Are you tired, happy, anxious? Then allow your mind to consider where you might be feeling anger in your life. Some sources may come right away—the neighbor who plays the stereo too loudly—but give yourself time to reach beyond your daily awareness. It's okay to talk to yourself.
4. Take a mental journey through the different worlds you visit in the course of a day—your spouse, your kids, your job . . . your boss, your coworkers, your employees . . . neighbors and community activities. Where does your anger turn up?
5. Write down any images or words that come to mind. Don't try to think too hard. This isn't about what you're thinking; it's about how you feel. Relax and open yourself to the images in your internal eye.

When the 15 minutes are up, review your list. Did you gain any new insight? Is anything surprising to you? Take note of any discomfort. As you go forward through this book, the discomfort may offer some important insights. This is an exercise you will want to repeat again and again as you grow more and more aware of your sensations, feelings, and thoughts.

Anger Isn't Bad, and Neither Are You

The first key in overcoming and understanding passive-aggressive behavior is to recognize that anger is a healthy, normal emotion.

It's an essential tool for navigating life safely and efficiently. In order to use it properly, you need to break free from the limiting beliefs you may have about anger. Perhaps you think that having any anger at all means you are a "bad" person. You may not want to look at certain childhood experiences that could possibly lend meaning to why you act the way you do. Or, maybe you don't even think you're angry. If you have any of these beliefs, I hope you'll just set them aside and read this book with an open mind. Here are some other myths about anger.

Myth: You have to be nice or people won't like you.
Reality: If you're always nice, people may start to wonder what you're *really* thinking, and begin to mistrust you.

Myth: Anger is dangerous—you'll lose control and hurt somebody or do and say something you'll regret.
Reality: If you learn how to respond to anger, you can take the danger out of it. If you let it build, you're more likely to explode.

Myth: Anger brings up issues that are too painful and uncomfortable to think about.
Reality: Unless you address these deep-seated issues, you will experience even more pain over time, and your relationships will suffer.

Myth: There's no upside to anger—it's all bad news.
Reality: By discovering why you're feeling angry, you can identify your needs and make mindful choices about what you want to say and do.

Myth: Anger is the death of relationships—and I don't want my partner to leave me.
Reality: When you examine your anger and express it mindfully, you open the door to better connections and greater intimacy in your relationships.

A lot of these myths deal with the impact of anger on relationships. The myth is that feeling our anger will *always* result in explosions that hurt the people around us. In our culture, in particular, the importance of "niceness" is overemphasized. From the time we're two feet tall, we're told to "be nice" to Grandma, Uncle Joe, little Peter, our teacher—the list is endless.

In the passive-aggressive loop, people draw the conclusion that if they aren't nice, no one will like them, and they desperately want to be liked, to belong. That's why they're also especially afraid of being angry with a partner. They don't want the partner to leave, and they're afraid that any anger, any conflict, will be the end of their relationship.

I would like to suggest here that anger is really the key that opens the door to intimacy. When we allow ourselves to feel our anger and assess its message, we learn important information about what we need to feel happy and loved. By sharing this information with our partner, we show our vulnerability—and that can feel dangerous—but it is also an invitation to that person to get to know us more deeply.

In too many relationships, each person is "in love" with her or his idea of what the other person is like. The reality may sometimes be painful, but it's the only route to be loved for your true self—and to love the other person's true self in return.

Anger and Passive-Aggression

Although hidden anger has many consequences, we're focusing here on passive-aggressive behavior. So how do you know if you're using passive-aggressive strategies to express hidden anger—or that you're dealing with someone who does? When anger is hidden, the best indicator may be what is *not* seen or expressed. If you don't feel or experience anger somewhat regularly, you should definitely consider the possibility that you fall into this group and pay special attention to the clues we're about to discuss. To find out if you or your partner (and, again, by "partner" I'm referring to any relationship, including a spouse, boss, coworker, employee, friend, or relative) suffers from hidden anger and passive-aggressiveness, answer the following questions.

Do you (or does your partner)—

- Withhold praise, attention, or positive feedback when someone else deserves or asks for it?
- Fail to follow through when a request is made?
- Stall when an important issue needs to be resolved?
- Withhold intimacy as a way to punish?
- Engage in sabotaging behavior?
- Respond with minimal words during important discussions? Examples of this are "Mm-hmm," "I don't know," "Fine!" and "Whatever!"
- Respond in sarcastic ways about life, herself or himself, or others?
- Feel frustrated, disappointed, or irritable a lot, sometimes without reaching the point of being angry?
- View most situations negatively, even when many aspects of them are going well?
- Frequently make small, negative comments that seem to undermine someone else's self-esteem?
- Feel depressed frequently or for a length of time?
- Never say no? (Or always say yes?)

If you answered "Yes" to any of these questions, this may be a sign that expressing anger is a problem for you (or your partner). Don't feel guilty—it's time to celebrate because acknowledging that anger is a problem is the first step toward resolving passive-aggression. Awareness of a problem is absolutely necessary for changing it, and sometimes it is even half the battle. With this key, you will start to become aware of your own anger or better recognize it in your partner when it comes up.

Anger Is a Healthy, Evolutionary Emotion

Human beings are always evolving as physiological creatures. I don't mean just biologically, but emotionally as well. Historically, the power boost that comes with anger has helped us to preserve our well-being and express our desires and needs.

Think of a baby. Lacking speech, lacking the means to move around and reach for what she or he wants, a baby cries. This is a primitive but highly effective expression of anger, and it usually brings someone to soothe the child and fulfill her or his needs. Some of these needs are physical—food, a blanket, a clean diaper—but others are emotional. Babies need to feel loved and connected to others. Man or woman, we've all felt the urge, when we see a small baby, to cradle, to cuddle, to coo. This basic instinct ensures that babies get the emotional comfort essential to their well-being.

As we grow up, we become more and more able to take care of our basic physical needs, but our emotional needs remain the same. We need to be safe and accepted, to be loved and to belong, to feel good about ourselves, to live with purpose, and to direct our lives toward our highest potential. When one of our needs is not being met, a built-in mechanism is triggered to let us know. This is the role of our emotions—anger, in particular. Our feelings serve as messengers, arising to deliver valuable information about our well-being.

Let's consider an example of how passive-aggression comes into play.

> Anne takes a seat at the conference table across from her partner. She checks again to make sure she has enough copies of the notes she assembled for today's meeting. Judy, the colleague who partnered with her on this assignment, already has her copy, so Anne has enough for the others, including the supervisor she's hoping will be impressed and give her a raise.
>
> When the subject of their research comes up on the agenda, Judy takes the initiative. Before Anne can pass out her notes or even speak, Judy is on her feet, using her iPad to direct a PowerPoint presentation. As Judy talks, Anne is surprised to hear some of her findings being discussed.

Sometimes her exact words appear on the PowerPoint image.

When Judy finishes, the boss asks Anne if she has anything to add. She is embarrassed; Judy has already said everything she planned to talk about. "I think Judy has covered our research very well," she says. "I have some notes, if anyone is interested." Judy waves her hand. "Of course," she says, "I've included Anne's findings in my report."

Anne is upset with herself. She looked stupid or lazy or both, she thinks. No one will ever know how much work she put into the project. As soon as the meeting adjourns, she slips out of the room, her notes still under her arm.

Anne has been robbed. If she had come home to interrupt a burglar in her apartment or been confronted by someone in a ski mask asking for her wallet, she wouldn't be upset with herself. She would see that a crime had been committed. In this case, there's no 911 to call. Anne has to be her own police force. Although she has a right to her anger, her behavior suggests a passive-aggressive approach to conflict. Standing up in the meeting and shouting, "I've been robbed!" would be justified but inappropriate and probably ineffective. Instead, Anne needs to feel her anger and take some steps to improve her situation.

> *"I think Judy's summary did a great job of offering a general outline of our work together. Of course, we've gathered a rich pool of data in support of those conclusions, and I've prepared some documents you can take away with you. You'll find some interesting nuances and details in them."*

Without criticizing Judy or calling her out for what she's done, Anne takes credit for her own contributions to their work and gives others in the work group—especially her supervisor—evidence of what she has provided.

By identifying your anger and exploring the feeling, you can hear the message it is sending and use it to improve your situation.

Exercise: Journal About Your Anger

Using a journal or notebook, monitor your thoughts and feelings for seven days. Record what you're thinking when you feel anger or discontent. Look for triggers—the types of things that set you off—and any patterns within your experiences and reactions. Also discuss the actions that you took or didn't take. For example, perhaps you ignored the feeling by pushing it down, or perhaps you engaged in another behavior as a way of distracting yourself to cope with the conflict. As you journal, be as honest as possible and take care not to edit yourself. Keeping your journal in a private place away from prying eyes will also give you the freedom to not censor yourself. The goal is to start becoming aware of how you handle situations that are uncomfortable.

Situation:

_____

_____

_____

_____

How I felt/What I was thinking: _____

_____

_____

_____

_____

What actions I took or didn't take:

_____

_____

_____

_____

Recognizing Anger in Your Life

I would like to reiterate that we *all* feel anger, and the fact that you do, too, doesn't mean that you are a "bad" person. It's just that somewhere along the way, you learned unhealthy ways of communicating that anger. Once you realize that you aren't inherently bad, flawed, or screwed up, that you're not inherently inept or deficient in relationships, you can begin to free yourself from the grip of your habits and start making new choices of your own design.

Where Did My Anger Habits Originate?

To understand hidden anger and the passive-aggressive response, it's important to know how the use of this tactic forms. More often than not, the strategy of avoiding anger and confrontation can be traced back to childhood experiences. Childhood development is the most crucial time for learning, and as we have already seen, it is the launchpad for passive-aggressive approaches to life. Children absorb information in a multitude of ways, but family is the most direct way that children shape their beliefs, attitudes, and behaviors. In general, there are three categories for how families typically deal with anger:

1. Anger-avoidant
2. Anger-expressive
3. Anger-healthy

Not everyone is firmly entrenched in one category, but these three types are a good place to begin looking at the style your family displayed when it came to anger.

- The *anger-avoidant* family type basically never expresses anger at all or acknowledges conflict, for that matter. Those who like to please others tend to come from these types of families. Only happy, safe feelings are displayed, and nothing "bad" is ever discussed.
- The *anger-expressive* family type is, on the surface, more dangerous. Anger is freely thrown around, and children learn to manipulate by being angry to get what they want. Often, love is shown through conflict or an explosive communication style.

- The *anger-healthy* family type reveals that relationships can have conflict *and* love. An argument or disagreement can occur, but at the same time trust, closeness, and affection are maintained. People respect one another and work together toward the mutual goal of resolving a problem and strengthening the relationship.

The importance of looking at which family style you came from lies in the reality that we take our childhood experiences into adulthood. We form patterns and then continue those patterns as adults, finding ourselves stuck, harming others, or, even worse, harming ourselves. To change our behaviors, we need to understand the reasons why we behave the way we do, as lasting change starts with awareness and ownership. While I'm not suggesting that we point fingers here—that's totally unproductive—it can reduce denial and feelings of guilt if we acknowledge that we came by our problems "honestly."

Exercise: Understanding How Your Style Developed

In this exercise, you describe how each of your parents or parenting figures handled their anger, as well as any messages they may have directly or indirectly given to you about how to handle your own.

1. How did your mother handle her anger? What messages did her words or behaviors send you about how to handle your own?
2. How about your father? What modeling or influential messages about anger did you receive from him?
3. Were there other significant people who demonstrated a way of dealing with anger that you adopted? What did you learn from them that shaped the patterns you use today?

Thankfully, it's never too late to learn healthy ways to express anger—as long as you're willing to live through the uncomfortable feelings that arise and examine their cause.

Early Warning Signs That Anger Is Building

If you are unaware that you have anger issues, there are warning signs that can tip you off. Few people understand that an impulse always precedes an angry reaction. Once you recognize this impulse, you can begin to identify your anger the minute it starts to arise. With this awareness, you have time to make a choice about how you want to respond to it, rather than taking the unconscious path that leads to passive-aggression. Partners of someone who suffers from passive-aggressiveness can use the same checklist to evaluate this person—and themselves.

Physical Clues

Anger, like all emotions, is a form of energy. The proof of this is in your body's reaction. Think back to the last time you got angry. Did you feel passionate, alive, invigorated? Probably. Adrenaline courses through our body as we start the fight-or-flight response. And while it's a little more challenging to identify anger if you have developed passive-aggressive tendencies (because you've learned to suppress the anger in the first place), there are some physiological clues that anger is building within you, such as:

- Tension
- Stiffening of something in your body (jaw, neck, hands)
- Feeling as if your heart has "dropped"
- Lack of appetite
- Headache
- Shaking or trembling
- Feeling hot in the face or neck

Behavioral Clues

- Pacing
- Tapping or stomping your foot
- Clenching your fist
- Raising your voice or changing its tone

Emotional Clues
- You want to get away from the situation
- You feel depressed, irritated, or guilty
- You are anxious around the other person
- You are overly critical or sarcastic when dealing with the person
- You engage in sabotaging or hurtful behaviors
- You purposely interfere with progress at work or in your relationships

Mental Clues
- Hostile self-talk
- Fantasies of aggression or revenge
- Obsessive internal thoughts about the issue
- Ongoing arguments with others about the issue

Exercise: Discovering Your Primary Anger Clue

1. Review the anger clues offered in this chapter—all of them, please, even the ones you're sure don't describe you.
2. Think of a situation when you felt angry and remember it in detail. How did you know you were angry? Does recalling the event trigger any sensations, feelings, or thoughts? Does your neck feel stiff? Are you feeling depressed?
3. Write down these responses—they're clues.
4. Think of other times when you were angry and repeat Steps 1 through 3, writing down clues as they come to you.
5. As you go through your daily routine in the next week, take a minute here and there to observe what's happening in your physical sensations, feelings, and thoughts. You may find it easy to identify the primary clues that anger is on its way.

Finding your primary anger clue is a cornerstone in the process of taking charge of your anger and choosing to explore it rather than react to it.

Stay With It

When you have symptoms like this, give yourself a few quiet minutes to explore your environment. What's going on around you? Who are you with? Have they said something that made you angry? What was it, and why was it a trigger? Many of the issues that make us angry have been with us from childhood. If, as a child, you were made to feel stupid or ugly or lazy—pick your adjective— you are likely to continue to respond with anger when someone or something awakens those old negative memories. They're painful, of course, but stay with them long enough to identify them and consider their source.

I know this is not the easiest thing to do. Anger makes us uncomfortable. The physical sensations can make it seem that we're moving toward violence—indeed, anger draws from the chemical fight-or-flight response, so part of its purpose was to prepare early humans for life-preserving combat. Today, we may experience road rage, which often leads to rash actions. That doesn't mean that such actions—or even explosive expressions of anger—are inevitable if we stay with our feelings for the time it takes to acknowledge them and look for their meaning.

Anger at those we love is perhaps the most distressing. How can we love someone and at the same time feel irritated and upset at what they've said or done—or not said or not done? It's just human nature. To build a strong relationship, we need to know what buttons our partner pushes. It's the only way we can have the kind of honest discussion that can help both of us deal with each other more sensitively. Without some emotional discomfort, followed by truthful self-examination, change and growth are impossible.

Advice for Partners

So far we've talked about the person with passive-aggressive behavior and issues associated with hidden anger. Those who are their partners, however, face related problems. Most people who are involved in passive-aggressive relationships describe their feelings as confused. Over time, this person who seemed so likable and easygoing, so pleasant and agreeable, is somehow provoking them to an anger they may at first ignore or fail to recognize. As time goes by, the pool of hidden anger builds, and inevitably, it is expressed, sometimes in irrational outbursts. In response to a request, for example, the passive-aggressive party may say a half-hearted "Sure," and suddenly the other person is shouting with rage. Beyond confusion and anger, partners may feel guilty about their actions and feelings and even start to question their own emotional stability.

At worst, partners may find themselves adopting the passive-aggressive response pattern. Consider this:

Phil is the head of a small work group at a marketing firm. The group meets every Friday at 3 P.M., and Dave never comes on time. There's a lot of grousing about the meetings among .the other four members of the group: By 3 P.M. on Friday, everyone is trying to clear the desk for the weekend, but holding the meeting at the end of the week is important. The idea is to wrap up what's happened and get ready for a fresh effort. Although Dave never complains, Phil can't help but wonder if arriving late—about 10 minutes, every time—is his comment. The meeting really can't get under way without him.

Dave's behavior enhances his isolation from the work group. While others can be seen chatting over coffee, providing feedback on each other's work, and even taking off for lunch together, Dave is always hard at work in his own cubicle. More than one of his colleagues snicker when Dave comes in late and makes his typical apology: an important phone call from a client.

On this particular Friday, Phil thinks he has the cure. He asks a colleague to send him an e-mail when he sees Dave leave his desk. Instead of going to the conference room, Phil waits in his office until the e-mail arrives, counts to 100, and goes down to the meeting.

Dave is just taking his chair when Phil arrives. "Sorry I'm late, guys," he says, making a point to catch Dave's eye. "I had an important phone call from a client—the guy you were just talking to, Dave. He said he hopes he didn't make you late for the meeting."

Everyone hoots at what they see as a practical joke, and Dave is flushed with embarrassment. Phil figures he's won this point.

But has he? Or has he just stepped onto the passive-aggressive merry-go-round? When partners begin to respond with passive-aggression to the passive-aggressive personality, the circuit closes on an endless loop in which no one ever says what they mean, and the stockpile of hidden anger starts to grow exponentially.

To avoid this outcome, partners need to cast aside the guilt they may be feeling about their anger and examine its sources. All of the exercises in this key are just as essential for the partner as they are for the person who has a history of passive-aggressive behavior. Recognizing anger is the best way to get to the root of conflicts in your relationship and deal with them effectively.

Exercise: Checking Your Responses

1. Find a quiet place where you can be alone and safe for at least 15 minutes. Relax—uncrossed arms and legs, shoulders down, feet flat on the floor.
2. Take a deep breath to a slow count of three and exhale, counting again: 1, 2, 3. Repeat until you feel calm and the urgent business of the day leaves your mind.
3. Focus on your interactions with your partner over the last day or two. The interactions that come first to mind are likely to be the ones that are still troubling you. Why? Were you uncertain about the meaning of your partner's behavior? Did it seem hostile or cruel, even if your partner's demeanor was pleasant?
4. Stay with your memory of the incident. See if you feel anger rising at the recollection.

5. Now examine how you responded:

- Did you agree or say yes because it was easier than arguing?
- Did you promise to do something and quickly forget about it?
- Did you forgive her or him, brush it off, and quickly forget about it?
- Did you feel the need to walk away?
- Did you reply in a subtle, humorous, or sarcastic way?

A "yes" to any of these questions indicates that you may be responding to your partner's passive-aggressive behavior by mirroring the same strategies.

With this book, I hope to help you come to an understanding of the dysfunction at the heart of your relationship so that you can explore your own hidden anger and find ways to address it. Passive-aggression is a game that requires a partner, and the outcome will surely be failure if neither party learns how to *break the rules*. That's what this book is all about.

To help you complete this important work of recognizing your anger, the next two chapters will examine this process more deeply. Your anger can tell you what's limiting you or missing from your life—you just have to listen.

KEY 2

RECONNECT YOUR EMOTIONS TO YOUR THOUGHTS

Linda and Franny were neighbors growing up in a suburb outside New York, and they attended the same K–12 schools, but they actually spent their childhood in vastly different worlds.

From her earliest years, Linda's family encouraged her to try new things, and they rewarded her efforts with affection even when she wasn't a complete success. Her parents told her she was a smart little girl and that her initiative and hard work would pay off. When she was disciplined—as all little girls at times need to be—her parents tried to explain what she had done wrong and how she could do better the next time. Linda grew up feeling that she could go to them for help with her problems and rely on them to understand and, most of all, love her.

Just a few doors down the street, Franny lived in a very different environment. Her parents were cautious people, and they were always warning her of the danger involved in "biting off more than you can chew." When she had trouble with a game or a toy—and later her homework—they told her that some people just aren't as bright as others. Her father sometimes called her "my little numbskull." Although her parents showered her with gifts, when she did something wrong they got angry and often took the gift away. If she got angry in return, they would take more things away. Franny learned to *hide her mistakes so that she wouldn't lose the gifts that were her biggest comfort.*

You may be surprised to learn that Linda and Franny got similar grades in elementary school. They had different learning styles, but both were above-average students. Still, Linda went on to university and a career in biotechnology. Franny figured she should start in a community college, and she ended up in a two-year program in computer science.

By the time they were 18, Linda and Franny had very different views of themselves and the world in which they would become adults. Linda saw authority figures as encouraging and helpful. She had strong self-confidence and was always willing to take a shot at building her skills and resources. Franny didn't trust authority figures—she was afraid that if she admitted a weakness or flaw, they would punish her. She figured she wasn't the brightest bulb in the box, so she limited her career expectations and boosted her self-esteem with new clothes.

Now, let's imagine they're shopping for a new dress, and this is what the saleswoman says:

"You know, that looks okay, but I'd like to see you try something else, too. Blue might be more flattering to your complexion. I think I have just the dress for you."

This is what Linda hears:

"I think you would look better in another dress."

She thinks:

"I'm so glad there's a competent saleswoman around to help me with this decision."

She feels happy to have the help.
This is what Franny hears:

"You look terrible in that dress, but then your complexion is the real problem. You have awful taste in clothes."

She thinks:

"Who does this woman think she is, giving me advice? Look what she's wearing! That's insulting."

She feels:

"She makes me feel ugly. I know I'm stupid, but I'm not bad looking, and when someone insults me, I get angry."

In the stories of Linda and Franny, you can see the impact of childhood experiences on the way we view the world and how we respond to our experiences today. While our physical skeletons are growing, we are also building a psychological skeleton, a framework we will use to judge situations and make decisions throughout our lives—or at least until we take the time to examine our thoughts and beliefs and see whether they are realistic.

You probably don't even realize you have such beliefs, and you certainly wouldn't consider them *opinions*—and yet that is what they are. We don't think of this thought structure as something we created. Instead, we view it as *the way things are*. To us, this is reality. If someone disagrees, he or she must be wrong. The problem is that sometimes *we* are wrong—what we see as reality is just a perspective that grew out of our childhood experiences: a set of beliefs.

Facts Versus Opinions

Facts	Opinions
Facts have an objective reality; they are developed by rational thought and examination of data; everyone agrees on their truth.	*Opinions are subjective beliefs or judgments; they are developed through personal experience and emotion; they vary from person to person.*

Today's high temperature was 82 degrees	It was much too hot. What a perfect day!
I scored 620 on the college entrance exam.	I'm brilliant. A lot of people are smarter than me.
Sandy just walked by me without smiling.	Sandy is angry with me about something. Sandy is awfully full of herself. Sandy seems preoccupied. I wonder what's up.
George is late for our dinner date.	George is never on time. George must be getting ready to end our relationship. George could have been in an accident. I hope he's okay.

Once the groundwork has been laid by belief systems that cause a child to respond in a passive-aggressive way, it isn't long before they are in a passive-aggressive loop, which affects all of the person's interactions.

These thoughts and beliefs intervene between what we actually experience and our response to those events. American psychologist Albert Ellis (1913–2007) developed an A + B = C model to explain this. In the equation A + B = C,

- A = the **A**ctivating event
- B = your **B**eliefs

- C = the emotional Consequences

It's clear in this equation that you're not responding directly to what happens (A). Your beliefs (B) intervene to influence your conclusions and consequences (C).

In Linda's case, the saleswoman's statement (A) combines with Linda's self-confidence and willingness to try new things (B) to produce her gratitude for the advice (C)—and maybe a more flattering outfit.

In Franny's case, the saleswoman's statement (A)—it's exactly the same words—is filtered through her low self-esteem (B) to result in reinforcement of her low self-esteem and anger (C)—but anger she will no doubt suppress, because her childhood has taught her that showing anger means getting punished. Note that Franny takes a mundane encounter and turns it into a stressful situation. This is a typical outcome when passive-aggressiveness is in play. Being afraid of our emotions puts people on heightened alert for problems or threats, which creates stress in almost any situation.

Now let's follow Franny's encounter with the saleswoman to see how this develops.

SALESWOMAN: *"You know, that looks okay, but I'd like to see you try something else, too. Blue might be more flattering to your complexion. I think I have just the dress for you."*
FRANNY: *"Actually, I like the cut of this dress [she fingers the fabric], but I'm not sure about the quality. Do you have anything similar in a better fabric?"*
SALESWOMAN: *"That's one of our best lines. Of course, I can show you some other things."*
FRANNY: *"That's all right. I'll look someplace else."*

Having misinterpreted the saleswoman's initial remark because of her self-limiting beliefs, Franny strikes back by disparaging the store's quality. This lifts her ego—she'll show the clerk who the fashion expert is. Then when the saleswoman challenges her, Franny decides to leave the store. Note that the saleswoman is probably pretty angry at this point, too—again, a typical outcome when passive-aggression is in play.

Unless this store is the only game in town, the passive-aggressive loop for this encounter will end here. When it appears in other relationships, as it often does, the passive-aggressive loop can have devastating consequences.

Through the stories of Linda and Franny, we've seen how people can develop different belief systems based on their childhood experiences. I call them belief systems, but people usually see them as The Truth. "This is the way the world is, how I am, and how people treat me." Those beliefs—built in the past—are a sort of lens that may distort how we view our present.

For those who develop a passive-aggressive personality, these thoughts and beliefs include some of Franny's issues: low self-esteem, mistrust of authority figures, sensitivity to criticism, and fear of anger. People who suffer from passive-aggressiveness also have a fear of *all* feelings, a tendency to see themselves as victims, and a focus on themselves to the exclusion of others.

The only way to break the passive-aggressive cycle is by uncovering these *irrational* belief systems. Because we created them, we can also change them if it turns out that they are limiting our growth as individuals or damaging our relationships with others. In this chapter, we'll look at the irrational beliefs that are most central to passive-aggressive behavior.

Fear of Anger and Other Feelings

So how do we identify these beliefs, if we actually "see" them as reality? In its role as a messenger from our boundaries of body and ego/self-image, anger can help us to identify our true feelings, and from there, we can look at the beliefs that would create such feelings and judge whether or not they are having a positive impact on our lives.

As we saw in Key 1, the problem is that most of us have learned that expressing anger is unacceptable behavior, and even as small children, we begin to stifle our angry feelings. This is certainly the mode of choice for people who adopt passive-aggressive behavior. There is no element more characteristic of passive-aggressive behavior than fear of anger.

To see how this happens, let's look again at Linda and Franny. As normal children, both no doubt did things that upset their parents—breaking something, making noise at inappropriate times, going someplace they weren't supposed to go—and anger is a *natural first reaction* for parents.

When Franny was disciplined, her parents got angry and took something away from her. If she got angry in response, they took more. As a result of this childhood experience, Franny will see anger and discipline as a precursor to loss. If someone disagrees with her, she will no doubt feel threatened. In classic passive-aggressive fashion, she will suppress her anger.

So am I saying she should cut loose, letting everyone see and hear exactly how angry she is? While this is certainly a choice—and some people make it—loud and even violent expressions of anger are not the only alternative. In fact, these eruptions are not the inevitable outcome when you choose to express anger. There is a third way.

When the child Linda was disciplined, her parents managed their anger and tried to explain why what she did was unacceptable. They talked with her about how she could do better and expressed their confidence that she would. In other words, they focused on the *behavior*, not the child. Because of her childhood experience, Linda is likely to see conflict as a time to sit down and discuss what went wrong and how it can be corrected.

Linda had the good fortune of having a childhood where anger was honored. A lot of people grow up in family settings where love and anger never coexisted, however, so they don't know how conflict and criticism can be expressed in a way that brings people closer instead of building walls between them.

Anger isn't the only feeling we learn to fear as children. U.S. culture puts a premium on optimism and cheerfulness. Think of all the sayings that underscore this. Big girls—and all boys—don't cry. In other cultures, people wail loudly at the death and funeral of loved ones. Americans admire people who don't display their grief, at least not with more than a quickly dabbed tear or two.

We cut ourselves off from painful and uncomfortable feelings, not just anger but also loss, fear, anxiety—"What, me, worry?"—and all forms of sadness. We do our best to present that serene and positive personality so admired—and richly rewarded—in our culture.

Unfortunately, when we cut ourselves off from our negative feelings, we also diminish our ability to feel all the positive ones that might give us cause for good cheer: love, joy, affection, satisfaction. Eventually, we become disconnected from our feelings to the point that we don't know what we really feel, and we therefore communicate only our thoughts—often irrational thoughts—about how we *should* feel or *believe* we feel. This is a very common side effect of passive-aggressiveness. Here's an example.

Dolores came to a therapy session bristling with unexpressed anger. Her husband's nephew was getting married in another state, she said, and he wanted her to go with him.

"Can you tell me more about this?" I said.

"Well, I won't know anybody there," she said, her rant picking up steam. "We never hear from his nephew—I'll have to buy the present and I know nothing about this boy. I have to decide what to wear, I have to pack for both of us, I hate flying. I'm going to make myself sick just thinking about it."

Then something insightful: "But Sam insists," she said. "He's just like my father."

As it happened, I had heard lots about Sam and about Dolores's father during her time in therapy, and they didn't seem to have much in common. I also knew that her passive-aggressiveness could easily express itself in physical illness. "Let's explore that," I said. "How are they alike?"

Before she could think, she blurted it out. "My father was always making me do things I didn't want to do." In fact, her father had been a prominent lawyer in her small hometown, and he'd had strong ideas about what little girls should do so that they would grow up into proper women—who would also do what they were told.

She was letting old anger at her father and his restrictions influence her response to her husband's request. While it was true that she might not see the nephew's wedding as a great event, making her husband happy by accompanying him was a positive action for her marriage. As we talked, she saw that it was really quite lovely that Sam—and his family, as it turned out—wanted her to be there for the wedding. It meant she was part of their family—a different perspective on the same request and one rooted in the present, not the past.

Like many people who suffer from passive-aggressiveness, Dolores longed for acceptance. Here it was right in front of her, and she had almost overlooked it because she was stuck in the past.

Reality Testing

My conversation with Dolores is an example of "reality testing." First, we looked at her husband's request and her thoughts and feelings about it. When we looked at what actually occurred, we saw that her husband and his wish that she attend a wedding with him had nothing to do with her father's rigid demands on her time when she was a child. Then we looked at the validity of the conclusion she had drawn—that he was imposing his will on her in an unfair way. Finally, she saw that indeed his request was not only reasonable but actually a lovely confirmation of her place at the heart of his family.

This "reality testing" breaks down into three steps, which we will look at more closely:

1. Identify my *real* feelings.

2. Assess their truth value.
3. Reconsider the encounter and react appropriately.

As you see, none of this would have happened if Dolores hadn't first expressed what she was feeling—anger—and explored what was causing her to feel that way (1). Only then could she check to see if she was assessing her situation correctly (2). Finally, she could reassess the situation and behave appropriately for this new reality (3).

What Am I Feeling?

Let's go back to Franny and see how this checklist might have helped her in her interaction with the saleswoman. First, Franny incorrectly identified her feelings. She thought she was annoyed at the saleswoman for her interference. Underneath that anger, she was feeling hurt: The woman seemed to be suggesting that she was unattractive and had no idea how to dress herself (1). Once she had really connected with her feelings, Franny could examine their accuracy. In fact, the woman didn't say she had a *bad* complexion, only that blue might enhance it. And she hadn't said anything at all about Franny's taste. All she did was make suggestions, which is what good saleswomen do (2). With her self-esteem back in place, Franny could have accepted the woman's advice—or at least could have considered her recommendations (3).

In the next key, we'll look more closely at ways you can get in touch with your feelings, even if they have been deeply buried for many years.

What's the Truth?

This can be the hard part because it often involves bringing to the surface wounds from childhood. Don't kid yourself that childhood is "long ago and far away," or that you're "so over that" childhood experience you still recall with fear. It's never over until you've examined the feelings and done the work that can help you heal.

Betsy is your classic Type A worker, a legal aide. Careful-ness is an asset in her job, but Betsy goes over everything 10 times looking for possible mistakes or oversights, and she snaps at anyone who interrupts her while she's "getting it right." In spite of all this, she's always anxious about her job perfor-mance. Most of the time, her boss has only compliments, but on the rare occasion when she criticizes something, Betsy is inconsolable for days. She goes over and over her work, trying to see how she made the mistake.

When people ask her why she's so hard on herself, Betsy jokes that her father thought the grading alphabet stopped with A. That's the truth, but it's no joke. Try as she might— and she tried mightily—Betsy could never do enough to win his approval. He could always find a mistake, even in her best work. It never occurred to her that he might have been "seeing mistakes" because he wanted to prod her.

As a result, Betsy had an anxious childhood. Her mother always left decisions to her father, so there seemed to be no alternative to just working harder. That's still what Betsy's do-ing.

Looking at your past is one way to find the truth.

Exercise: Revisit Key Childhood Experiences

1. Find a quiet place where you can be alone for 20 to 30 minutes.
2. Take with you something that you can use to record your thoughts and feelings—a journal, a tablet, a laptop.
3. Settle yourself with a few deep breaths.
4. Close your eyes and think back to your childhood. Which emo-tions do you remember seeing as you grew up?
5. When people were sad, what did they do? What about when they were anxious?
6. How did your family deal with grief?
7. How did your parents respond when you got angry?
8. How did your parents respond when you cried?

Another way to find the truth is to look at it from outside of yourself. Examining other potential points of view is a way to get a rounder view of yourself and your issues, and it's particularly useful for people with passive-aggressive personalities and their partners. It's an indirect—but highly effective—way of finding out what's on someone else's mind.

> *Thanksgiving is just around the corner, and this is the year they're supposed to spend the holiday with Sue's family. Henry is dragging his feet about going, and Sue is sure it's because she has a brother Henry really dislikes. The last time they spent the holiday with her parents, the two of them had a fight. Henry insists it's not that, but he doesn't seem to want to talk about it. Sue has often been too tired for lovemaking for a few weeks now, and Henry has started to wonder whether there's someone at the office she's seeing when she "works late," which is often.*
>
> *When she comes home after 11 o'clock one night, he explodes and accuses her of infidelity. Sue is so shocked she blurts out the truth: "I've been working extra overtime so I can take the kids and go to my parents' house for Thanksgiving—you can just stay home if you don't want to go."*
>
> *At last they sit down to talk. It turns out that it's the cost of the four plane tickets to the faraway home of Sue's parents that has had Henry concerned. He's started looking at what they have in the bank, and he's worried about paying college tuition when their oldest child is ready for school in a year or so. As it turns out, Sue's overtime has resolved the problem for now—there will be more than enough money for everyone to go. And they decide it's time to check in with each other more often about what's actually on the other person's mind.*

Considering what the other person might *really* be thinking is an important way of getting to the truth of the matter. If your partner forgets something from the grocery list, does this really mean she *never* pays attention to what you want? Could it be that she lost the list? Or the price was too high? Or she simply forgot? If you feel you're carrying too much of the workload, is your boss *always* making demands? Does he know that you feel overworked? Are other people doing as much as you're doing? Have you asked for help?

Exercise: Opening the Discussion

In the case of Sue and Henry, the truth was blurted out in an argument, but finding the truth about other people's feelings can be done in a more structured way. The next time you have a conflict with a partner or colleague, ask him or her to play a game with you. Each person takes a piece of paper and writes down what he or she thinks the problem is. Then you trade.

This is a particularly useful exercise for couples in a passive-aggressive relationship. You might make it a regular feature of Friday dinner. Each person can write down what he or she thinks has been going on with the other. Then trade. Then talk.

The trick to finding out the truth is to ask for it honestly. Tell your wife (or whomever you are asking) that you honestly want to know. Tell her that whatever the answer is, you and she will be better off knowing the truth.

In Henry's case, it would certainly have hurt if Sue was seeing someone else, but at least he no longer would be deceiving himself. And like Henry, you might learn that your beliefs are false and that your wife does want to be with you.

Let's try another case. Suppose you think you are particularly unattractive. This is a tougher one to check out, but certainly not impossible. If you ask someone if you are unappealing, likely you will not get an honest answer. And if you tell someone to answer you honestly, you are putting that person in an uncomfortable position. But what you can do is tell whomever you are asking that you are on a quest to look the best you can. Say you are looking for suggestions about how to improve your "curb appeal." Ask for what suggestions she has. If you present the question this way, you will surely get ideas.

Reconsider the Encounter

Let's revisit the office encounter in Key 1 and do some reality testing. You'll recall that Phil was the head of a marketing work group at a marketing firm. His problem was Dave, a member of the team who was always late for a crucial Friday meeting, always with the same excuse: He had a phone call from an important client. As Phil saw it, Dave thought he was better than the rest of the team. He never hung out with the other members, never participated in feedback sessions, never socialized. Being late for the meeting was just another way of saying, "I'm more important than you are." Phil dealt with the problem by arranging to arrive even later than Dave on one particular Friday and making a joke of Dave's tardiness.

Sad to say, Phil had totally misunderstood the situation. Dave actually felt intimidated by the group. When he was a kid, his overprotective mother had kept him away from most team activities, and she had also had unrealistically high expectations of him. Dave was late every week because he had to psych himself up to go. He was always afraid he'd say the wrong thing and embarrass himself. As a result of Phil's passive-aggressive strategy for responding, this never came out, and Dave's embarrassment at the joke made his isolation—and productivity— even worse.

Other Faulty Thinking
Typical of Passive-Aggression

It's amazing how many households, how many families, function day to day with no expression of feelings. Besides anger, we also struggle to ignore or hide our anxiety, our fear, our sadness. Faulty thinking hides our true emotions from us. Here are some typical patterns of faulty thinking among people with passive-aggressive personalities:

Self-Flawed or Telescopic Thinking	Nothing I do is good enough. I am inadequate/unworthy/ unlovable (choose your adjective). I always feel like a failure. There's something wrong with me—I don't care what people say about my positive traits.
Perfectionist Thinking	I have to do things perfectly in order to be satisfied. I can't accept any flaws or failures.
Blurred-Boundary, Self-Victimizing Thinking	I might feel that I'm overworked or unappreciated, but I will never say no. My husband/wife/boss/friend expects too much from me. It's just one demand after another, and they never seem to see how tired and stressed I am.
People-Pleasing Thinking	I want everyone to like me. The more approval I get from others, the better I feel about myself.
Pessimistic/Resistance Thinking	I'm overwhelmed by the amount of work and stress in my life, and it seems I'm always fighting for the smallest thing. I often despair that the situation will ever get better. This is life—at least mine.
Helpless Thinking	This is not the life I was hoping for. I'm running from one end of the day to another, taking care of the house, the kids, the boss. Everybody dumps on me, and I resent it, but what can I do?

These thought patterns may be hiding your true feelings—including anger. You'll notice how many superlatives are in these descriptions: *nothing, always, never*. If your thinking is reflected here, it's time to consider what's *actually* going on.

The Victimhood Mentality

Because holding on to relationships is so important to them, people who suffer from passive-aggressive behavior may suppress their anger and negative feelings to the point where they become chronic victims. If something goes wrong, they're quick to take the blame. And they would sooner jump off a cliff than say no. They might as well be wearing a T-shirt with "Dump on Me!" in big red letters across the chest.

Some people feel that being the victim or martyr is the only way they can get attention. By doing *everything* the other person asks, however, they tend to create reservoirs of guilt and eventually anger in their partners rather than the gratitude they expected. In the meantime, their needs continue to be unmet—they haven't asked for anything, so they surely won't receive anything. And deep inside, their own reservoirs of anger and resentment grow. Nobody is truly happy in this situation.

If this pattern sounds familiar, you should know that it doesn't need to be permanent. Next time someone asks for a favor, however small—even a cup of coffee—make yourself take two deep breaths before you answer. You need to stop yourself from instinctively—and passive-aggressively—saying yes when you might really want to say no.

Take a moment to evaluate the request or the invitation before you answer. Is this something you want to do? If not, take a chance and say no. You don't need to make a large explanation.

> "Sorry, I can't take on that job right now. My schedule is too full."
> "You know, I'm not a big football fan, so I'll pass on the tickets."
> "Thanks for thinking of me, but I can't."

When you say yes when you want to say no, you might avoid a confrontation, but you're hurting yourself and you're building an expectation in the other person that "yes" is what you'll say all the time. If you don't set and respect your own boundaries—something we'll take up in Key 4—you can't expect anyone else to do it for you.

For example, if someone asks me to go to an event over the weekend, I will consider a number of things before responding:

- Is this an event I want to attend?
- Do I enjoy spending time with this person?
- Do I have other obligations for the weekend that might conflict?
- How is my energy level? If I have a heavy workload during the week, I might need some private time over the weekend to recharge.

Self-Centeredness

People often do not understand that their passive-aggressive behavior is the source of their trouble. They see the world from a single focus: themselves. If someone becomes angry with them, they are puzzled and hurt.

> *Marty and Kate work together at a bookstore. When Kate comes in one morning, Marty asks for a favor. "We have a bunch of new used books to shelve in fiction," she says. "I know you probably have other things to do, but could you handle that?"*
>
> *"Sure," Kate says.*
>
> *"It's important. Soon as you can, please."*
>
> *Kate looks at the messages on her desk and makes some phone calls. A couple of people have asked for information about books in her nonfiction sections, and it takes time to track them down. Then it's lunchtime.*
>
> *When she comes back, Marty is at her desk again, loading the unshelved books onto a cart.*
>
> *"I don't know why you say you can do things," Marty says, "if you don't have the time."*

Kate is surprised at Marty's anger. "I didn't think it was that urgent."

Marty shakes her head, angrier now. "I said soon as you can."

"Yes, and that's what I was doing," Kate replies. "There were some things on my desk I needed to clear up, and I got involved. I'll do the shelving right now if it's that important. I don't know why you're so mad."

"Forget it," Marty says, stalking away from Kate's desk with the books.

There are a couple of cues to passive-aggressiveness in this example. (1) Kate gave a knee-jerk "Sure" to Marty's request without considering what her agenda was for the day. She didn't ask what the timeframe should be for this favor; she just said yes. (2) Kate delayed implementing the request. She drifted from one chore to another through the morning, then went to lunch without attending to it. It didn't even cross her mind. (3) When Marty got angry, Kate had an automatic excuse—"I didn't know it was urgent"—when really she could have figured that out if she'd been listening.

Breaking the Loop

The kind of faulty thinking patterns involved in passive-aggressiveness don't serve you well. When you allow these irrational beliefs formed in childhood to determine your behavior as an adult, your road through life will be unnecessarily rocky. Your relationships will be damaged, and you will leave behind you a trail of frustrated and confused partners.

But let me repeat. These are beliefs you created, and so they are beliefs and thought patterns that you have the power to change. The next time you find yourself in an upsetting situation, take a couple of deep, cleansing breaths and relax. Here is a process that may help you reach a positive outcome.

Step 1: Describe the situation.	What happened? Who was there? What did they say or do? What did you say or do?
Step 2: What is my reaction?	What is upsetting you? What thoughts are running through your mind? What are your emotions? What physical sensations are you having?
Step 3: Reality Check.	What are the bare facts of the situation? What would an impartial observer see and hear? Which facts support your reaction? Which facts suggest you are reacting incorrectly?
Step 4: Look at the other side.	What is the other person likely to be feeling? What emotions is he or she expressing? What are they saying? How do the bare facts support or undermine them?
Step 5: Consider outcomes.	What alternatives do you have? Which one would best serve your needs and boundaries and those of the other person? What would be most helpful overall? What have you learned from this exercise about the thoughts and feelings you had when it started?

As you proceed through these steps in different incidents, you may want to keep a journal. Over time, you may see that you are gradually identifying and discarding beliefs that are unhelpful in your relationships and life.

Exercise: Change Your Mind

When irrational beliefs created in childhood are determining your adult behavior, you may find that your mind and its thoughts are your own worst enemy. You can use this exercise to identify the thoughts that are sabotaging your happiness, success, and well-being. That knowledge can help you change your mind from enemy to friend—and improve your life.

1. Review the list of faulty thinking types listed in this key. Which patterns are closest to your own behavior? Write them down, leaving plenty of space around each item. This is a good time to be rigorously honest with yourself.
2. Underneath each thinking type, answer this question: "How does this make me feel?" For example, what body sensations and emotions do you experience when you think of yourself as unworthy, inadequate, or unlovable?
3. Consider how you developed this belief. Did someone tell you? Did you decide based on his or her behavior?
4. Now explore the opposite of each belief. If you think you are a failure, write down your successes. If you feel powerless, pretend that you have control of your life and write down what you would do. As you write down these opposing statements, pay attention to how you feel. Is anything shifting inside you?
5. Go back to the original statement. Ask yourself, "Is this a belief that is helping my happiness or success?" If not, remove the original statement from your list.
6. Consider what you might do differently to change this pattern. What type of thinking would promote your success and happiness? You have the power to change.
7. To ground this new choice, make a table with two columns, with

the old belief on the left and the new belief on the right. Post it someplace where you can check it easily. If you find yourself relating to life in the old way, read your new thought and observe the change in how you feel.

Old Thought	New Thought
Playing and having fun are a waste of time.	Taking breaks to play and have fun recharges me.

Advice for Partners

Suppressed feelings are so commonplace in our society that I believe this key can help anyone to improve their own emotional and mental health—and as a result their satisfaction with all aspects of life. For partners of those with passive-aggressive personalities, there are special challenges.

You have no doubt felt angry at times about behavior your partner has displayed that seems bewildering. Reality checks for you mean trying to find the truth about what he or she is doing. If your wife turned up late for dinner, was she doing it on purpose to make you anxious and angry? Was *she* angry about something? What explanation did she give, and does it have the ring of truth?

When dealing with passive-aggressive behavior, you may need to challenge your partner's behavior and its motives. "I have the feeling something else is going on here. Can we talk about it?"

Sometimes you'll be having what seems to be an ordinary conversation when all of a sudden your partner becomes agitated or defensive. You may have inadvertently touched on an issue from the partner's past that triggers an uncomfortable feeling. Devoting a lot of time to figuring out what you said or did that was wrong will be unproductive.

Think of Dolores's husband, Sam. All he did was ask his wife to attend a nephew's wedding. It didn't seem like such a lot to ask—he was even hoping they might turn the trip into some fun sightseeing. Sam could have thought for weeks about what was upsetting her without striking on the truth. She was upset because his request reminded her of the unreasonable demands her father made when she was a girl living at home.

When situations like this arise, it's important to consider that you may have nothing at all to do with your partner's response. If possible, talk about it. Otherwise, let go of your guilt. This is not your fault.

Here are some characteristics of people who have developed passive-aggressive behavior patterns.

- Impulsiveness and low tolerance for frustration
- Irritability
- A circular dysfunctional relationship with someone in one's life
- Low energy and passiveness
- Resentment
- A history of unhappiness and seeing life as a struggle
- Low self-esteem
- Emotional or verbal abuse

A breakthrough in your relationship can come once you understand and accept the hurdle that passive-aggressiveness represents to your relationship and can openly discuss the issue. In this approach, you need to call the person out on his or her passive-aggressive behavior and press for a response. In the following example, a couple is working hard to deal with her lack of empathy and chronic reliance on passive-aggressive behavior.

> On Fridays, Natalie and Billy like to go out for lunch—a relaxing break at the end of the work week. On one particular Friday, they are both caught up in tasks related to their small business—paperwork, unexpected phone calls, employee problems—and Natalie especially is running late. It's 2:30 by the time they get to the car.
> Billy tells her that he's starving, to the point of feeling sick and even seeing white spots in front of his eyes. She em-

pathizes and tells him she'll drive to the restaurant as quickly as possible to ease his discomfort. After a moment or two, however, a song comes on the radio and Natalie finds her thoughts drifting to the project they're working on. Billy's hunger is quickly out of her mind. The freeway is fairly open, and the restaurant they're heading for is about 15 minutes away.

While she could pass the car in front of her, Natalie doesn't—content to go with the current flow of traffic and her thoughts. Billy says angrily, "Come on, pass this guy. Let's go!" Natalie glances at the speedometer and responds with an excuse/rationalization that occurs to her right then: "I don't usually go faster than 70. I don't like to speed."

Billy, who is keenly alert to her passive-aggressive ways, calls her out on it. "That may be true," he says, "but you were just coasting along and not thinking about my need to get some food quickly." Normally, Natalie would be defensive and stick to her original excuse, but she is becoming aware of her passive-aggressiveness and wants to change it. She looks honestly at what she did and decides that he is right.

She is embarrassed to admit it, but within minutes, her empathy for his feeling sick had disappeared and she had been driving along in her own world, unaware of the semicrisis that was going on for him. She was devoid of empathy in that moment, and her actions reflected it.

She decides to share her thoughts with him, confessing what happened. To her great surprise, Billy's anger immediately calms. Despite the unpleasantness of the situation, and how much he would like to be treated with empathy without having to get angry and ask for it, he is pleased that she didn't continue to make excuses and be defensive and instead took ownership of her thoughts and behavior.

Exercise: What's Happening Here?

This exercise, based on the reality-checking steps listed earlier, can help you get at the reality of what's happening in an interaction affected by passive-aggressiveness.

1. Find a quiet place where you can be alone for 20 or 30 minutes. Take along some paper or a digital device that will let you record your thoughts and feelings.
2. As objectively as possible, describe the situation. Exactly what did each person say or do? How would an outsider describe it?
3. How did you respond? What upset you? What were your physical sensations, emotions, and thoughts during the encounter?
4. How did your partner respond? Did he or she seem upset? From what you could observe, what were his or her physical sensations and emotions?
5. What do you think was going on? Re-create what you think were the partner's thoughts and feelings during the encounter.
6. Look at the evidence. What do the facts—both from the incident and your history together—suggest about what was happening?
7. Share the findings of this exercise with your partner and give him or her a chance to respond.

In this chapter, we have looked at how irrational thoughts developed in our childhood may be hiding our true feelings from us. We saw how these belief systems influence the way we see the world and respond to others. Finally, we learned how we can examine and assess these belief systems and begin to discard those that are not promoting our success and happiness. In the next chapter, we learn some techniques for reconnecting with our sensations and emotions.

KEY 3

LISTEN TO YOUR BODY

This is the second marriage for both Meg and Tim. Her three children from the first marriage live with them, and Tim's two children visit two weekends a month and four weeks in the summer. While Tim works two jobs to pay their bills, Meg does everything related to the house and children, and she also handles customer service phone calls—working from her kitchen—for a couple of local businesses.

It's a lot of work, but Meg never complains. Her first husband left her, and she's determined to keep Tim—she doesn't notice that she never complained during her first marriage either, and he still left. When it's just the household, her own kids, and the job, Meg feels stressed, but she can hold things together. When Tim's kids arrive for the weekend, it's another story. Too often, Tim is gone for much of their visit, so she's left wrangling five kids on her own. His children are not as well behaved as hers are, and she figures she'll get in trouble if she disciplines them.

Lately, their visits have been making her sick. The headache starts a few hours before they arrive, and her stomach will hardly hold down any food while they're around. One weekend, she called a babysitter and took to her bed. Tim was furious, so now she's decided to leave them on their own, and part of the time she doesn't know where they go. If they're not around when she serves dinner, she lets them fend for themselves. She envies Tim's ex-wife, Georgia, who uses her child-free weekends to play with her new boyfriend. While her kids

are spending August with Tim and Meg, Georgia is taking a
vacation in Italy. Meg doesn't know how she'll survive a month
with five kids.

Meg is clearly disconnected from her feelings, and it's not difficult to see the passive-aggressive loop in her behavior. Instead of talking with Tim about the workload related to his children—or at least asking him to participate in their care—she's just letting the work and her anger pile up. Leaving them on their own is not an appropriate solution—they're children. Notably here, she's also ignoring what her body is telling her. Those headaches and the nausea are screaming, *You need help! You need to examine the feelings you're ignoring and do something about their message.*

In the last chapter, we saw how people are often taught at a young age that negative emotions—especially anger—should never be expressed, and we learned how that contributes to passive-aggressive behavior. In this chapter, we're going to see how our body can help us out of this dilemma, if we're only willing to pay attention. First, let's see how we can enhance our well-being by getting in touch with our emotions.

Emotions Are Messengers From Our Sense of Self

Emotions are a gift that tells us how our environment is affecting us. They let us know when our boundaries are being violated or our needs are being left unmet so that we can make things better. If we ignore our emotions—and that's a big feature of the passive-aggressive loop—then things stay the way they are: bad.

The Defining Role of Boundaries

People have boundaries to protect their physical body, their ego, and their identity—each person's is different. Healthy boundaries help us to feel safe in the world. When any of our boundaries are violated, we feel threatened.

Say you're taking a walk, and a teenager is coming down the sidewalk toward you on a skateboard. He's watching his feet so he doesn't see you, and he has earbuds in both ears, so he won't hear you warn of a collision. You just barely get out of the way, although his arm knocks into your chest and you lose your balance for a minute. You probably feel a rush of tension through your body—the fight-or-flight response that was built into our brain's hardware when we still lived in the forests and things went bump in the night.

This same reaction follows psychological as well as physical threats, and it has become a leading cause of illness. High blood pressure, ulcers, and cancer have all been linked to the fight-or-flight response. Scientists have shown that ongoing stress promotes aging and illness.

Obviously, Meg's headaches and nausea indicate that her physical boundaries are being crossed—she's working too hard— but her ego boundary is also under fire. Disrespect—for Meg it comes explicitly from Tim's kids and implicitly from him—is damaging to our sense of self-worth. This boundary also has evolutionary roots. Maintaining the respect of the tribe was essential to survival. Finally, Meg's self-image is at risk. It's clear that she values her role as a wife and mother. In these circumstances, she's starting to fail at that job.

When their ego or self-image is threatened, some people might lash out in response and defend themselves vigorously. That's not the passive-aggressive way. Sulking or withholding affection are some passive-aggressive strategies for dealing with boundary violations. Physical symptoms are also part of the repertoire.

Exercise: The Last Time You Got Angry

1. Find a quiet place where you can be alone for 10 or 15 minutes. Think about the last time you got angry.
2. Picture the event in detail. What words or actions made you angry? Was someone else involved, or were you angry at yourself?

3. Looking at the discussion about boundaries, see if that explains your anger. Was there a threat to your physical boundaries? Or was it a violation of your ego? Was your sense of self harmed, threatened, or disrespected?

4. Did you express your anger? If so, how? If you didn't express your anger, what did you do?

5. Take some time to explore your anger and understand its causes. This can have huge benefits.

Identifying Unmet Needs

Emotions also help us identify needs that are not being met. Besides food, clothing, and shelter, we have many emotional or social needs. It's common in the passive-aggressive loop that you become so focused on your own needs that you don't see what's happening with others around you. This checklist of key emotions offers a way to inventory your own needs and also to consider what's happening with people close to you.

Attention	Because you are important to me, I'm focusing on you and what you're saying.
Affection	We like to express our warm bond with hugs and touches.
Appreciation	I know how much you've added to my life, and it makes you even more important to me.
Acceptance	I understand that we all have positive and negative traits, and I recognize who you are while offering you the space to grow.

Reliability/Accessibility	You are always at the head of my list: When you need me, I'll be there to listen to your feelings and address your needs if I can.
Responsiveness/Engagement	I see this as a continuing connection between my heart and yours. I'm not going anywhere.

Exercise: Identifying My Needs and Meeting My Partner's Needs

1. Take the checklist and find a quiet place where you can be alone for at least 15 minutes.
2. Review the list and see if any of these are unmet needs in your life.
3. Using pen and paper or a digital device, write down your unmet needs. What could your partner do to improve the situation?
4. Now think of your partner. What could you do to meet these emotional needs for her or him? Make a list—this is brainstorming, so the order doesn't matter.
5. Once you have a list, you can organize it into a plan. Make sure you check back to see how you're doing.
6. Share your own identified needs with your partner and suggest ways she or he could make you feel more emotionally safe.

What Happens to Emotions When You Don't Listen

There are consequences that must be faced when you suppress your emotions and fail to listen to their message. Because anger is such a crucial piece of the passive-aggressive loop, let's start there.

Unless we evaluate and release it, anger never goes away. It turns up as passive-aggressiveness and other self-defeating behaviors, habits, addictions, and even illness. When we can't manage our anger, we lose our voice—and with it our self-esteem and self-respect. Instead of protecting our boundaries and asking for what we need, we let other people make decisions for us. Intimacy can't be achieved without honesty, and we're not being honest.

Too often, parents—uncomfortable with anger themselves— teach their children that anger is never to be expressed. Children may not see their parents get angry—or maybe the anger is always loud and hurtful and frightening. Either way, kids are going to look for a solution to this uncomfortable feeling.

The False Self

Often children will develop a "false self," creating the son or daughter that they think their parents and other adults will accept and love. It's an ingenious coping skill, providing survival resources to get us through difficult situations when we're children. But if we maintain it as adults—when it's no longer necessary—the price tag can be catastrophic. Inside a false self, we become more and more separated from our true feelings. Instead we're operating like a puppet all the time, doing and saying what "the good girl" or "the good boy" would do or say. These youngsters often grow up as "the helpers," "the people pleasers," and "the martyrs" who inhabit the world of passive-aggression. Meg is a classic martyr—and a classic false self, one that probably started growing in her childhood and is blocking her from any true sense of her feelings.

But while the false self is never angry, the "true you" has to deal with all that repressed anger. If we stuff our feelings out of sight, then we also hide who we are. To others, we may seem shallow because all the feelings that would give us depth and character are tucked away.

The Cost of Shame

Preventing children from expressing their feelings also creates shame—shame about the way they feel and shame about their insecurity and their confusion over how to express it. In the passive-aggressive personality pattern, you will find a reservoir of shame beneath the defensiveness, rationalizations, and excuses that are so quick to be used.

People feel guilty because they think they've done something wrong. Shame is a feeling that comes about when people believe they themselves are wrong. Because children can't separate their feelings from their self-image, when they experience bad feelings, they come to the conclusion that *they* themselves are bad. So, while guilt arises when you have made a mistake and can fix it, shame develops when you see yourself as the mistake—believing that *you* are bad. Perhaps because they don't know how to deal with the tears, parents often encourage their children to "stop crying." Whatever has made them unhappy, the children are told, "is nothing to cry about."

Until We Process and Release Our Feelings, They Reside in Our Bodies

When you're stuck in a passive-aggressive loop, the most natural response to feelings is to stuff them out of sight. This wouldn't be so bad if your psyche were like a tunnel and the discarded feelings would just slip harmlessly out the other end. Instead, the psyche is more like an expanding bag. Until you examine the feelings, retrieve their message, and let them go, they remain in the bag. For some people—those with passive-aggressive personalities in particular—the bag can get pretty swollen. It's a heavy burden to carry around; think of all the energy you're using up to do that.

The body deals with physical wounds in a rather straightforward way, with a series of healing steps. Say you cut your finger: Blood vessels tighten to reduce the volume of bleeding, and platelets or clotting proteins are the first responders, working to seal off the injury from the rest of the body. White blood cells arrive quickly to destroy any germs or toxins. It hurts for a while, but in no time at all, new skin cells grow over the wound, and eventually the scar is gone.

Like the body, the psyche knows what needs to happen to heal emotional wounds. When we stuff them away in the bag, however, that healing process cannot begin, and the longer they fester, the more harm they can do us. Whenever similar events happen in our lives, the old emotions emerge and cause us pain — trying to get our attention — until we resolve them. They *want* to be healed. As long as we keep suppressing them, they will continue to hurt.

An important first step in the healing process is to sit with emotions — especially anger — long enough to hear what they want to tell you. I'll be asking you to do just that. Believe me, I know how hard this will be for people stuck in the passive-aggressive loop. But I also know that if you don't sit with your anger and other emotions — if you don't take them out of the bag, feel them thoroughly, and let the healing process begin — they will return to cause you pain and to sabotage every relationship you try to build. You'll find yourself making choices that re-create the circumstances that caused the original injury. If you had an abusive parent, you'll find yourself drawn to one abusive partner after another. That's how it works.

The best thing we can do for our children is to raise them in an environment where it's safe to express feelings and speak the truth to each other. That's the only way to give them a secure home — where the kids are not always trying to figure out how their parents are feeling and what they truly want. Parenting styles that suppress anger and other emotions send kids off into adulthood with a psychic bag already bulging with repressed feelings. Worse still, they've never learned how to deal with their anger, respond to the underlying messages, and use what they've learned to bond together more closely with the people they care about.

The Body Doesn't Lie

The good news for those of us stuck in adulthood carrying this kind of baggage is that all the information we need to begin healing is still with us. Besides bearing the scars of our physical injuries, our bodies also register experiences like anger, fear, and sadness. By experiencing our body sensations and their related feelings, we can recover and reconstruct the past in order to set ourselves free from it. The body has a wealth of information for us—and it never lies. Listening accurately to our bodies, we can build new habits for approaching our feelings. A new response strategy will replace the passive-aggressive pattern that may have dominated our life.

The key to this is mindfulness, which can help us to embrace the truth of our experiences—including anger and other painful emotions. The techniques of mindfulness make use of your body and its sensations as a key to your rich inner life: impulses, feelings, sensations, thoughts, and beliefs.

Listening to your body can help you:

- Understand when your boundaries are being crossed so that you can take appropriate action
- Become more conscious of your needs—once you know what you want, you can ask for it
- Identify painful emotions—understanding them will lighten that bag of suppressed emotion that has been sapping your energy
- Reveal your thoughts and beliefs—recognizing what they are will help you let go of those that aren't contributing to your well-being

With time and with mindfulness practice, you'll get more and more in touch with the internal information that is available to you, including:

Body sensations and muscle tension
Emotions and moods

Thoughts and beliefs
Memories and mental images
Worries and judgments
Impulses and urges

This is the road to a more honest and satisfying life; it is the key that can open the jail of passive-aggressiveness.

What Is Mindfulness?

Think of the word *absent-minded*. You get an image of someone meandering along, misplacing belongings, getting lost, forgetting about vital tasks, losing track of conversations. I imagine Mr. Magoo, although his basic problem was near-sightedness. Still, he bumbled through life, virtually unaware of what was going on around him. A good pair of glasses would have helped Mr. Magoo, and I believe that the practice of mindfulness can do the same thing for you.

Mindfulness is a practice in which we intentionally focus on the present: on where we are and what we see, hear, think, and feel. Although, as human beings, our minds often drift to the past or the future, in mindfulness, we stay in the present. The idea is not to be preoccupied or distracted by anything that leads us away from the intensity of the moment. Another important element of mindfulness is to observe our thoughts and feelings *without judging them*—that way we avoid a reaction that could lead us away from the present because of our discomfort with the feelings.

Buddhists use mindfulness to reach a higher consciousness. They want to avoid "going through the motions" without paying much attention to what's going on around them. Buddhist practice also includes looking at our present situation with curiosity: What are we feeling, and why?

Many people operate at an entirely different level. Obsessed by the past and anxious about the future, they may hardly ever catch the full impact of what is actually going on now. When you go through life unaware of what's happening inside you, you can lose sight of how you might be contributing to your own problems. On the one hand, you will ignore your anger and other feelings, but you will also miss out on a lot of life's pleasures and joys.

Embracing Mindfulness

If you hope to change the passive-aggressive loop that character-izes your life, mindfulness is not only a tool but a responsibility. Whatever the passive-aggressive framework of your thoughts has told you, you are *not* helpless or a victim of the choices others make. You have the free will and the power to change the way you view the world, paying full attention to your behavior—not just what you do, but what you think and feel. This will help you re-spond appropriately to your anger, and that is a key step in moving away from passive-aggressiveness.

All right, you say, but how can you get there from wherever you find yourself now? Think of it this way: You've already made a start. When you find yourself aware of the present—drawn by a beautiful sunset or a powerful emotional experience or just a quiet moment—take time to notice how the buzz of distracting thoughts disappears, how connected you are to your senses, how alive you feel. Now accept it as your responsibility to do this more regularly. Over time, you will train yourself to be mindful. Here's an exercise that will help.

Exercise: Practicing Mindfulness

1. Find a quiet place where you can be alone for at least 10 minutes.
2. Sit comfortably with your arms and legs uncrossed, your hands relaxed in your lap, your feet on the floor. Take a couple of slow, deep breaths, counting in your mind—one, two, three—as you inhale and exhale.
3. Quiet your mind and let thoughts of the past or future drift away. Closing your eyes may help.

4. Once you are calm and focused on the present, open your eyes and look around, paying attention to the sights and sounds in your environment. What do you see? Colors, shapes, textures, size? What do you hear? Is there a clock ticking? Are you hearing music or traffic noises from outside your space? If you have a beverage, take a sip and feel it as it passes down your throat to your stomach.
5. Thoughts about the past or future may try to emerge. Acknowledge them but go back to deep breathing until you are calmly focused on the present moment again.
6. Simply enjoy this time and place and the feelings of your body.

Take a mindfulness break a few times each day—it's easy to do. With time and practice, you will find that you can bring mindfulness into your daily routine. Instead of listening to the radio in the car, pay attention to the people and neighborhoods you pass— and of course, keep your eyes on the road. Or focus on the mechanics of driving: how the steering wheel feels under your hand, how the car responds to pressure on the accelerator. Instead of turning on the TV while you're fixing dinner, focus on the shapes of the ingredients, the smells and sounds of cooking.

Try to cut back on multitasking. If you just slow down a bit— your movements, your speech—you'll find it so much easier to focus on what you're doing *now*—and this will help you become more aware of your experience in the present.

Another way to develop a habit of mindfulness is to give yourself some reminders. Leave sticky notes in the car, in the bathroom, near your laptop or tablet, in your wallet. You might add a message—"Be here now"—but just seeing the note will remind you to take a quick, quiet moment to check in with yourself. "Where am I right now?"

Sensations: The Language of the Body

Through mindfulness, you can connect with the sensory experiences of your body, which is the first step in using mindfulness to discover and understand your emotions and thoughts.

Our senses—sight, hearing, smell, taste, and touch—get physical stimulation from our environment—for example, brightness or noise, or the rich smell of brewing coffee. Our sensations are the physical feelings that result. Sensations also reflect what's happening in our internal organs—hunger or fullness, pain or pleasure. Sensations are the language, the words, your body uses to communicate with you: "I'm chilly," "My leg hurts," "That's hot."

Following is a partial list of sensations and words that describe sensations. You can probably think of additional examples.

Sensations and Words That Describe Sensations

Beating	Expansive	Nauseated
Blushing	Faint	Numb
Breathless	Fast	Obstructed
Bruised	Fatigued	Open
Burning	Floating	Painful
Chilly	Flooding	Pins and needles
Clammy	Flowing	Pinching
Clenched	Fluttery	Pounding
Closed	Freezing	Pressure
Cold	Full	Pulsating
Confused	Goose bumps	Queasy
Cool	Hard	Quivering
Cramping	Heavy	Relaxed
Crushing	Hollow	Released
Damp	Hot	Scratchy
Decreased	Hungry	Sensitive
Dissociated	Immobile	Serene
Distorted	Increased	Shaky
Dizzy	Inflamed	Sharp
Dry	Inflated	Shuddering
Dull	Invigorated	Skittish
Effervescent	Itchy	Slow
Empty	Knotted	Smothering
Enlarged	Lifeless	Soft
Exhausted	Light	Sore
Expanding	Limp	Spasm

Spinning	Swollen	Tingling
Squeezed	Taut	Trembling
Stabbing	Tender	Twisted
Stiff	Tense	Twitching
Still	Thick	Unsteady
Stimulated	Throbbing	Vibrating
Stinging	Tickling	Warm
Sweaty	Tight	Weak
		Wet

Now I'd like you to experience some of the subtle and perhaps not-so-subtle sensations that your body is using to speak to you.

Exercise: Observing Body Sensations

1. Make a mental inventory of your body—head, check; shoulders, check; ears, check. Avoid places that are injured or painful.
2. Stop at the place where you typically hold everyday tension and focus your attention there.
3. What sensation do you feel? If you can't find the right word, use the list we just reviewed. Does your stomach feel queasy? Is your eye twitching? Do you have tightness in your head or neck?
4. Write down what you sense.
5. Stay focused on this body part for five minutes or so, without doing anything to change the sensation. Does it change anyway— just because you're paying attention to it? If it changes, find a word that describes the new sensation.
6. Write down what you sense.
7. Did you need help naming your sensations? That's okay. You may have trouble identifying and naming your sensations at first.

Like the basic mindfulness exercise, this one is great to repeat as often as you can—or you can just take a minute to check in with your body's sensations, trying to name each one with a single word. As you grow more skilled, you will become more tuned in to what your body is saying—and that will set you on the road to exploring your real experience.

Using Mindfulness to Get in Touch with Your Emotions

So far, we've used mindfulness in a simple and nonthreatening way. We've slowed down and started to pay more attention to our internal and external environment. Now we can use this tool to explore our internal self—thoughts, feelings, impulses, and memories. This will feel more threatening, particularly to those who have a fear of feelings and memories. Yet this voyage of self-discovery is the only road to emotional healing and to eliminating passive-aggressiveness from your life.

Sensations are not the same as emotions. While sensations are physical responses, emotions are states of consciousness. Sensations and emotions may come at the same time, but that doesn't mean they are the same thing. For example, if you're angry, you might feel a fast heartbeat or a headache. Tightness in your chest is a sensation; anxiety is an emotion.

But while sensations are different from emotions, they can help put us in touch with our emotions, including anger, that we might not notice otherwise. When we practice mindfulness, we choose to listen to what our body is saying about our internal activities. This is the start of breaking the passive-aggressive pattern.

Emotional mindfulness lets us experience and address the emotions we feel in our body as they are happening. If you're stuck in a passive-aggressive loop, you may want to run in the other direction, but you need to get up close and personal with feelings, especially those that are painful. To open yourself to a more honest and intimate lifestyle, however, you need to accept this passing discomfort with the understanding that, as with a hurt finger, the pain means healing is under way.

Feelings: Your Friends

We can explore our emotions by connecting them with sensations so that our body will help us reconnect with our feelings. Body language, behaviors, and words can help us get internally focused on our experience.

The exercises in this chapter will help you to go slower, to be reflective about yourself and your environment. You'll be present in the moment. By *present*, I mean that you will be fully in your body. When we are afraid or upset, when the world around us seems unsafe, we tend to retreat. This is particularly true of people caught up in passive-aggression. To properly protect ourselves, we need to be present during challenging situations, even if it's uncomfortable or threatening. It's the only way to be true to ourselves and fully inhabit our lives.

Expanding Your Feelings Vocabulary

One way to become fully present is to be aware of your sensations and emotions and to name them. We have already learned words to describe sensations and tried to sit quietly to identify our own. When you enlarge your emotional vocabulary, you'll have a more nuanced sense of your feelings and an improved knowledge of yourself. In addition, you may get a more precise understanding of what others are experiencing so that your empathy grows—a good direction for those with passive-aggressiveness.

I've divided emotions into two groups: (1) the positive emotions (the ones we find most comfortable), like joy and love, as well as the negative emotions (the ones we generally dislike), such as anger and fear. If you've been engaged in passive-aggressive behavior, your knowledge of positive emotions may have been limited by your suppression of the negative ones. That's because when we cut ourselves off from feeling certain emotions, we limit our ability to feel them all.

Let's look at both, and as you do, see if you can think of times when you've felt them. Then, try to recall the physical sensations that went with the emotional experience.

Words That Describe Comfortable/Positive Feelings

Happiness/Joy	*Enthusiasm*	*Love*
Blissful	Alive	Adoring
Bubbly	Ardent	Affectionate
Buoyant	Avid	Amorous
Carefree	Breathless	Caring
Cheerful	Dynamic	Cherishing
Content	Eager	Compassionate
Delighted	Earnest	Doting
Ecstatic	Encouraged	Empathetic
Elated	Excited	Enamored
Enthusiastic	Fervent	Enchanted
Euphoric	Gung ho	Fond
Excited	Hopeful	Forgiving
Festive	Intent	Grateful
Giddy	Keen	Infatuated
Glad	Motivated	Kindly
Inspired	Powered up	Open
Jolly	Spirited	Passionate
Jubilant	Zealous	Romantic
Lighthearted		Seductive
Merry		Sensual
Optimistic		Sentimental
Peaceful		Sexy
Playful		Soft
Pleased		Sympathetic
Satisfied		Tender
Silly		Treasuring
Thrilled		Warm
Upbeat		

Words That Describe Uncomfortable/Negative Feelings

Anger	*Hurt*	*Sadness*
Agitated	Aching	Crestfallen
Aggravated	Battered	Defeated
Annoyed	Bruised	Dejected
Belligerent	Crushed	Depressed

Anger (continued)	*Hurt (continued)*	*Sadness (continued)*
Bitter	Devastated	Despairing
Boiling	Distressed	Despondent
Brooding	Injured	Disappointed
Contemptuous	Pained	Discouraged
Cross	Shamed	Dismal
Disgusted	Suffering	Down
Displeased	Torn	Dreadful
Enraged	Tortured	Dreary
Frustrated	Wounded	Dull
Fuming		Forlorn
Furious		Gloomy
Grumpy		Glum
Hateful		Heartbroken
Heated		Heavyhearted
Ill-tempered		Helpless
Incensed		Hollow
Indignant		Hopeless
Inflamed		Impotent
Infuriated		In the dumps
Irascible		Inconsolable
Irate		Melancholy
Irritated		Miserable
Livid		Moody
Mad		Morose
Mean		Mournful
Miffed		Out of sorts
Offended		Passive
Pissed off		Powerless
Resentful		Somber
Riled		Sorrowful
Upset		Unhappy
Vengeful		Useless
Wrathful		Weepy
		Woeful
		Worthless

Confusion	*Fear*	*Worry*
Ambivalent	Afraid	Alert
Baffled	Alarmed	Antsy
Bemused	Daunted	Anxious
Bewildered	Desperate	Apprehensive
Dazed	Fearful	Distrustful
Disconcerted	Fidgety	Doubtful
Disoriented	Frightened	Hesitant
Distracted	Horrified	Ill at ease
Indecisive	Hysterical	Insecure
Lost	Intimidated	Nervous
Mixed up	Panicked	Questioning
Perplexed	Paralyzed	Skeptical
Puzzled	Petrified	Suspicious
Spacey	Scared	Tense
Wavering	Shaky	Uneasy
Wishy-washy	Shocked	Uncertain
	Startled	Uptight
	Surprised	
	Terrified	
	Threatened	

Exercise: Naming Your Feelings

1. Find a quiet place where you can be alone for 15 minutes or so.
2. Using the mindfulness strategies you learned, get centered or grounded—that means being in your body. Stand with your feet a comfortable distance apart, right below your hips. Notice the support you get from the floor or ground. Relax, bending your knees slightly, so the surface can carry all of your weight. Really feel how the surface supports you.
3. Now pull your shoulders back and take several slow breaths in and out. Massage your arms, neck, and shoulders and feel the responding sensations.

4. Recall a time when you were angry, and review the details until you feel that emotion and its accompanying sensations. Say, "I am angry." Repeat it different ways—louder, softer; faster, slower.
5. Pay attention to how your body responds.
6. See what other feelings come up. As you feel them, name them out loud: "I am afraid. I am sad. I am feeling lighter now."
7. When you have named all of the feelings you notice, relax and take a few more deep breaths.
8. If you'd like, write about what happened. "It's safe to be present in my body," you might say. "It's safe to feel my feelings."

Doing this exercise will give you a lot of information. For one, you'll learn about how you feel regarding owning and expressing your anger and other feelings.

Roadblocks to Mindfulness

Don't be discouraged if mindfulness doesn't come easily at first. Here are some typical problems and possible solutions. At first you may feel anxious or resistant to exploring your emotions. I know this is a big hurdle for people with passive-aggressive personalities, but I also know that you can succeed.

If you sit for a couple of minutes with one of the exercises and then decide *nothing* is going on inside you, please persevere. Your sensations and feelings aren't used to having your attention, and they may be a little shy. What's five minutes? Promise yourself to sit for five minutes each day and sincerely try to connect with your inner life. I think you'll be rewarded, and the eventual impact on your life can be extraordinary.

A key requirement is to give up control. Just relax and see what comes up for you. Don't start writing scripts for your inner life or steering the first sensations that arise toward the conclusions you'd like. Just be curious and objective. And remember that mindfulness is not about judging. None of your feelings are "bad," and there's no shame in feeling them.

You also have to be willing to change. If you have a history with passive-aggressiveness, you probably know a lot of the power of silent resistance. There's some comfort in the irrational beliefs and preconceived narrative you have about yourself and your life. But it's a cold comfort or you wouldn't be reading this book. You want to change. You can change. And you'll be happy you did.

Perpetual Mindfulness

Very soon, you'll see the effect that mindfulness can have in your life and how it can help you break the bad habits of the passive-aggressive loop, something we'll delve further into in Key 7. When you approach each moment without a lot of filters—remember those irrational beliefs formed in childhood—you'll see yourself and your life more clearly. You'll also begin to make a better connection with partners, children, and other people in your life.

Maybe you think mindfulness has to be practiced in a darkened room with New Age music playing and incense burning. The truth is, you can practice mindfulness wherever you are, whatever you're doing, any time of day or night. Eventually, you may find that you're simply *being* mindful. All of the time.

But mindfulness is especially important when you're facing a confusing or troubling situation and you need to get a good grip on how you feel. It can also help you to move through uncomfortable thoughts and feelings. Through mindfulness, you can understand how you are reacting to a situation and get in touch with those feelings. Being mindful actually changes the way your brain processes emotions. In that new mode, you can learn to:

- Slow your responses so you don't simply react to triggers
- Experience distressing emotions like anger so that you can receive their message
- Avoid unhealthy coping strategies like denial and avoidance
- Focus your thoughts in the present without judging them

- Open yourself to new experiences and new ideas about changing your behavior

If you find yourself living inside the shell of a false self, mindfulness can help you break through that shell and liberate the real person within. You may have thought you were only lovable if you were quiet, cheerful, funny, clever, obedient—you pick the adjective. Now you have the opportunity to reclaim the pieces of your identity you left behind. Whoever you are is just fine.

Advice to Partners

Once you identify a partner as having a problem with passive-aggressiveness, it's easy to feel a certain amount of relief: You're not crazy after all—or at least, if you are, it's because you've been *driven* crazy by your partner. To say that a partner is in a passive-aggressive cycle does not, however, make you a paragon of mental and emotional health. This book can be just as useful to you as to your partner with the target problem.

What You Can Do for Yourself

Getting in touch with your feelings—and staying in touch with them—is crucial to maintaining stability in a relationship—*any* relationship, but especially one facing the challenge of passive-aggressiveness. This key has some sound exercises to help you understand how to clear out the confusion that a passive-aggressive partner can create and zero in on what you're feeling.

Because of the way passive-aggression works, we may be inclined to pull our punches emotionally. "I shouldn't be upset—she was just a little bit late." Or, "Why do I feel angry? He agreed to do what I asked. There's no reason to be angry."

While you are rationally analyzing your partner's behavior and making excuses for it, however, your body will be telling you the truth about the situation. If a partner's behavior makes you uncomfortable, pay attention. On the positive side, you may think, "He looks so enthusiastic about helping me with this—I bet he'll do a great job" or, "She seems really happy, so we'll have a nice evening."

What You Can Do for Your Partner

Particularly in relationships where you *and* the person who has a passive-aggressive personality have agreed on the problem, you may be able to help your partner identify feelings and examine their sources. Body language is a useful tool here—although it provides only one message, and not necessarily the message your partner will recognize or act on.

I recently saw a play, *Seminar*, about a writing class in which the teacher disparages everything his young would-be authors do. Their body language is full of anger, but they don't express it to the teacher. Instead, they rail on and on with each other without going to the source. And oh, yes, they go to bed with him, too. An entirely different physical message.

Still, understanding some body language associated with hidden anger may help you understand your partner's emotions—even if he or she doesn't. Some of them are fairly obvious. Yes, clenched fists and crossed arms indicate aggressive or defensive postures that the person may not recognize. Also, people tend to look down when they're upset or trying to hide something emotional. A hug can tell a lot: Passive-aggressiveness often expresses itself through rigidity, a body that seems to resist and is uncomfortable with contact.

If you notice these body signs—and your own body is telling you that something is wrong—it may be useful to try to open a discussion. We'll talk about how to do this more in Key 5. An important rule, however, is to describe it from your point of view.

"I feel uncomfortable with the way
you're looking at me. It feels like anger."

not

"You're angry at me! What's going on?"

"I'm concerned that I said something to upset you."

not

"You look like you're upset. What did I do?"

And don't speak at all until you've identified your own feelings and are in a comfortable place emotionally. You want a conversation, not a confrontation.

In this key, you've learned how to get in touch with your sensations and feelings. These lessons will help you to identify the physical and emotional boundaries you set to keep yourself feeling both separate and secure. We explore that next.

SET HEALTHY BOUNDARIES

*K*aren and Ray have been living together for six months after a year of dating more and more exclusively. To Karen, moving in with Ray had seemed a natural development in their relationship, but six months later, she still isn't sure how Ray feels.

When they were dating, Ray was always saying—usually when it was time for her to go home after spending the night with him—that it would be so much nicer if they shared a place. When Karen's lease ended and her landlord raised the rent, she told Ray this seemed like the right time to do it. He agreed, and he seemed enthusiastic, but then he added that he was traveling for work half of the time anyway, and it was a shame that he was paying rent while the place stood empty. She was hurt by this pragmatic comment, but she decided to ignore it.

Other things about the relationship bothered her. When Ray was traveling, usually two to three days in a row, she moved things around to make herself more comfortable—not furniture so much as kitchen things, her favorite cup—and she put some of her own knickknacks and books out. After he was home a day or two, everything would be back in the original place; Karen's stuff was pushed into a corner. It hardly felt like her place at all.

Karen kept a grocery list on the refrigerator in the kitchen, but when it was Ray's week to shop, he would forget to take it, or he would just overlook the items on the list that were her *favorites and not his. If she invited her friends for dinner, Ray would always turn up late or sometimes not at all: "I'm sorry, sweetie, but it's business. You'll have your friends anyway, so you won't miss me." But when they went to parties with his friends, he kept her so close it was as if his belt were wrapped around her waist, too. All of his friends told her Ray had never been this involved with a woman. They were sure a wedding was in the future.*

Karen was not so certain. One day, she saw his suitcase in a corner of the bedroom—he never put it away, even if he was home for more than a week at a stretch, as if he might leave at any moment—and she exploded. By the time Ray got to the bedroom, she had pulled her own suitcase out of the closet and started packing.

"What are you doing?" he asked.

"I'm leaving," she yelled. "You don't want me here anyway."

"Sweetie! How can you say that?" He tried to hug her, but she shoved him away and kept packing. "No, please. You can't go."

And then he was sitting cross-legged on the floor in the doorway, his face in his hands.

"Ray?"

"I need you so much. Please don't leave me."

So, she didn't.

Although she would figure it out soon enough, Karen hadn't yet realized that Ray was deep into passive-aggressive behavior. Boundary issues play a key role in passive-aggressiveness. People with passive-aggressive personalities have only the vaguest sense of boundaries. Particularly in relationships, they may find it hard to distinguish between *I* and *you*. But as we can see here, boundaries are also a problem for the partners of those with passive-aggression. Karen is living in Ray's apartment, but it's hard to say whether Ray is *living with her* in any real sense. She is implicitly accepting his lack of boundaries and losing her sense of self—and her self-esteem in the relationship.

Blurred boundaries are among the faulty ways of thinking adopted by people with passive-aggression, as we learned in Key 2. We have also seen, in Key 3, how our emotions are messengers from the front lines of our boundaries, telling us something is wrong. In our story, Karen is getting messages from her emotions—her confusion about how Ray feels, her sense of being unwanted, and finally her anger—about boundary violations. But she's not yet listening.

Boundary issues are a crucial element in relationships where at least one of the partners is stuck in a passive-aggressive loop. In this chapter, we'll see how both players will benefit from examining how well their own boundaries are formed. First, let's see how healthy boundaries work.

What Are Boundaries?

Boundaries are the invisible lines that draw our self-identity. In Key 3, we saw that boundaries affect three major areas: physical, ego, and self-image.

Physical Boundaries

An exercise I often do with my patients reveals physical boundaries at their simplest: personal space. I ask my patient to stand, and I walk toward them. I ask them to tell me when they feel uncomfortable, but it's usually pretty obvious from their body language. Crossing arms, averting eyes, even stepping backward.

Physical boundaries also embrace our enlarged personal space—our office or bedroom, our belongings, and our openness to body contact. An earlier generation found a handshake between nonrelatives to be the limit of affectionate contact. Today, full-body hugs are common among acquaintances—same sex and opposite sex. Mouth-to-mouth kisses are usually reserved for potential sex partners, however, at least in the United States.

Healthy physical boundaries play an important role in sexual contact, as well: how much is permitted and under what circumstances. "PDA" has become the code word for the public display of affection, and there's a fair degree of individual variation in what constitutes an acceptable PDA.

Ego Boundaries

The exercise I do involving physical boundaries often reflects something about ego boundaries, as well: the amount of intimacy a person comfortably accepts. A healthy ego includes private spaces where only some people are admitted and only under some circumstances.

We might tell our best friends things about our background we would be unlikely to share with neighbors or coworkers. In other words, healthy emotional boundaries shift according to the person we encounter and our relationship. Say you have a big presentation coming up for your job. Its success or failure will have a major impact on the company's profits and your own career progress. To your best friend, you might admit that you're scared to death and won't be able to eat until it's over. To your colleague, you might say that you know a lot is riding on your effort and ask him to wish you luck. To your boss, you might say that you've worked very hard in preparation and you're ready to go.

We might also set boundaries *against* information that will cause us unproductive emotional upset. I've seen women respond quite differently to a breast cancer diagnosis. One woman bought a highly regarded book by a medical doctor that described every facet of the disease; she read it cover to cover three times. Being thoroughly informed eased her fear. Another woman bought the same book but only read bits; she would use the index to isolate information that affected her and read only that. Going beyond, she felt, brought her imagination into play—what if this happens?—and she had enough to fear already.

There's a difference between healthy ego boundaries and emotional walls, which are a way to keep our distance. Healthy boundaries are flexible and may change depending on the person or the circumstances we encounter. Their goal is protection. Emotional walls are rigid and are intended to isolate. Wall makers are legalistic, intolerant, and governed by rules. The difference is indicated by the words *never* and *always*. These superlatives are often part of a wall: "I never make friends at the office." A boundary would more likely say, "I am cautious about engaging in too much intimacy with colleagues, and I am watchful to see if emotional connection might interfere with our professional tasks."

Self-Image Boundaries

Most of us have a self-image that reflects what we value in ourselves and how we see our role in our family, our workplace, or society in general. A woman who takes great pride in the appearance of her house will be sensitive to any criticism, while a woman who sees herself primarily as a mother might not care what you say about her house—but don't say a negative word about the kids! Still another woman may love her kids but have her self-image invested in her career. If she loses her job, the kids may not be a consolation.

Self-image includes qualities as well as roles. An Episcopalian who values his spirituality will not like being told by a charismatic Baptist that his religion is too secular—and in reverse, the Baptist doesn't want to hear that his beliefs are superstitious.

Defending the Boundaries

Anger is the soldier on patrol along healthy boundaries, letting us know when they're being attacked. Its weaponry is the fight-or-flight response built into our brain. If we're attacked, or in an accident, or in danger from a storm, the fight-or-flight response pours chemicals into our brain that prepare us to defend ourselves or run away. It gives us a burst of energy.

People who are in touch with their feelings recognize their anger and pause while they check on its source. Then they decide what words or actions would be the best response to the perceived threat. If someone is sitting too close to you on the train, you might ask her to give you more space, or you might simply look for another seat. If your partner has said something that seems critical about your appearance, you could point this out to him, or you could decide to just let it go. The important thing is to acknowledge the anger and consider your response.

Many people, however, are afraid to express anger and stuff those feelings out of sight—not just everyone else's sight but even their own. For those with the passive-aggressive pattern, this becomes standard procedure. Anger is something they want to avoid at all costs, so they ignore the related sensations and feelings, and they miss the message the emotion might be sending. In relationships, people who are passive-aggressive also fear that if they try to set limits, their partner will leave. As a result, their boundaries are virtually undefended, and after a while they lose all meaning.

Having weak boundaries opens them to everything from outright physical abuse to being overburdened with work or just being taken advantage of by others. Those with a passive-aggressive personality try to protect themselves in indirect ways, for example, by withdrawing. In our opening example, Ray quietly pushes Karen's books into the corner rather than dealing with his uncomfortable ambivalence about having her things in his place. Unable to assertively ask for what they need, people with a passive-aggressive personality will use manipulation, though largely unconsciously.

As you'll recall, passive-aggressiveness generally begins in childhood, sometimes with outright abuse or with a domineering parent who withholds the acceptance children crave. There's a powerful fear of conflict and loss—reflected in Ray's collapse to the floor when Karen threatens to leave. It's a manipulative tool—he gets her to stay by playing on her emotions and her guilt, without really addressing and correcting the issues that are creating a distance between them.

The result of this experience—and the passive-aggressive behavior it spawns—is a growing pool of hidden anger. Instead of telling Karen he really likes to have the coffee mugs on *this particular* shelf, he quietly puts them back when she moves them someplace else.

Establishing good, clear boundaries reduces anger. Boundaries can reduce stress, anxiety, conflicts, and misunderstandings. Believe it or not, they can also increase connection and comfort. Once we know our own boundaries and those of our partner, we can develop sensitivity to the boundaries of others and a willingness to respect them. Some people are more comfortable than others with affection or with shared emotions or shared space, so we respond by developing an implicit map of their boundaries. For example:

- Greg isn't a hugger. You can grab his elbow when you shake his hand, but that's the limit.
- I went into Jackie's desk once looking for scissors, and I could tell she was really upset about it. Now I try to remember to ask instead of helping myself.
- Ted is a lawyer, and he's really sick to death of all the bad-mouthing lawyers get. I try to keep this in mind when we chat.
- Cherie doesn't like to talk a lot about her feelings—at least with me—and there's only so much about my feelings that she's ready to hear.

Statements like these may seem strange to people living in a passive-aggressive cycle. They tend to be low on empathy, so they probably haven't even noticed the other person's boundaries—or if they have, they conclude that the other person is overly sensitive and the one with the problem.

Characteristics of Weak Boundaries

For people caught in the passive-aggressive loop, boundaries may blur or even overlap. Here are some examples that will probably be familiar to you.

- *You don't protect your private space.* Although it may make you uncomfortable, you allow people to stand much closer than you'd like, to touch you in a familiar way, to enter your personal areas—rooms, drawers, computer files. People who hug you may feel your resistance, but you say nothing.
- *You dislike being alone.* Faced with the prospect of being at home on your own for an evening, you're likely to call friends and invite yourself along on an outing. Anything to have company.
- *You reveal too much.* It's okay to share your feelings with a close friend, but the clerk at the drugstore probably doesn't need to review your love life with you.
- *You get caught up in other people's feelings.* If your brother loses his job, you feel the anguish and distress. Sometimes you're so caught up in other people's troubles that you are more distressed than they are. The key here is that you're not really sharing *their* feelings. You're playing out a drama, and they're just providing the script.
- *You neglect your own needs for the sake of others.* Anything someone asks—you're ready to do it, even when it conflicts with what you need. In our introductory example, Ray asks Karen to stay, so she does, even though she's hurting in this situation.
- *You engage in sex when you don't want to—even on a first meeting.* When the other partner wants sex, you feel that you have to comply. You're likely to have sex on a first date—a relationship is either sexual or it doesn't matter.
- *You confuse sexual attraction and love.* You're constantly falling in "love at first sight" because you can't distinguish between love and infatuation.
- *You tolerate abuse.* You're afraid to resist, so you let a spouse or partner abuse you emotionally or even physically.
- *You are easily persuaded by one religious group or another.* When you were a child, you adopted your parents' religious beliefs—or lack of them—without question. The unquestioning approach continues into adulthood, making you highly impressionable and easily persuaded by a variety of spiritual ideas or groups. For example, you'll open the door to an evangelist, frequently adopt

a new faith group, or become overly attached to the leader of your church—without using much discernment, if any at all. You often give your power away, assuming everyone else is wonderful or knows better than you do.

What Boundaries Tell Us About the Origins of Passive-Aggression

It's not hard to see breached boundaries in the symptoms of passive-aggression. In fact, such violations are at the very heart of passive-aggression: childhood abuse; the imbalance of power in the parents' relationship, where one parent was subservient to the other; a too-rigid parent crossing the ego bounds of their children by demanding too much and failing to show respect for them and their emotional needs; and parents who showed a lack of acceptance for their kids for one reason or another—again landing a blow of disrespect against the child's sense of self.

People who don't develop strong boundaries during their developmental years often become passive-aggressive adults. They suffer from low feelings of self-regard and don't feel that they deserve to have their needs respected. Of course, they still experience anger at the violations, self-neglect, and intrusions that they allow, but they suppress the anger. It tends to leak out in sabotage, insults, chronic lateness, forgetfulness, or other tactics, provoking arguments and straining friendships. Even the person who is using these revenge-like tools may not know that's what's going on.

Dependency Issues

People caught in a passive-aggressive loop often struggle with an internal conflict related to boundaries: They desperately depend on someone else for acceptance, energy, and attention, yet they also fiercely desire independence—a narcissistic desire to do things "their way."

Ray is a good example of this. He wants Karen to live with him, but he doesn't make her welcome. Deliberately or not, he treats her like a guest in his house, and maybe one who is staying too long. Yet he's torn up when she threatens to leave because he relies on her for acceptance and safety—he doesn't like being alone. When he's traveling, he often stays in the hotel's bar or restaurant until it's nearly empty. He often picks up women companions, and Karen would be especially wounded to know that they sometimes go back to his room with him.

People suffering such a conflict may be indecisive and verbally defer to their partners. While the partner seems to carry all the responsibility for making all the decisions, it may feel like a hidden or ulterior agenda is playing out beneath the surface. Although Ray had often suggested that Karen move in with him, she was the one who made the final decision—and he's seemed uncomfortable with it ever since.

The origins of this conflict also lie in childhood. A key phase in child development packs an emotional wallop: "separation/individuation." As children become more independent physically—they can move around and play by themselves—they go through a stage where they begin to see themselves as more than an appendage to "Mom" but not yet quite "me." You've probably seen this in a store or other public place. The kid is exploring the territory happily until someone speaks to him—then he runs for Mom and glues himself to her leg.

Unsure of themselves, children are torn between a genuine inclination for independence and the need for their parents' protection. They may roam around for short periods of time, but they'll check regularly to make sure Mom is where they left her. The roaming expresses the wish for freedom, the checking, an acknowledgment of dependency on a familiar and trusted figure.

Parents wrestle with this issue, too. Given too much freedom, children may put themselves in danger before they know how to respond. Given too little, they may never develop the skills they need to function as adults. People who are caught in the passive-aggressive loop fall somewhere between the two extremes of dealing with freedom, and they continue to have conflicts and fears related to dependency. Whether they're 3 or 30, 6 or 60, they remain at heart scared and insecure, always looking for Mom but resenting her intrusion at the same time.

Of course, even the healthiest relationship includes elements of dependence. Implied, however, is that two fully independent adult people choose a relationship in which they depend on each other—all the while knowing that they can take care of themselves. Dependence then becomes a sort of gift: I trust you to take care of me without impinging on my right to be separate. I choose our mutually dependent relationship freely, not because I'm afraid of being alone or can't get along without you.

Boundaries When Passive-Aggression Is the Third Party in the Relationship

You can see that setting healthy boundaries is an important step in overcoming passive-aggressive behavior. If you are in a personal or professional relationship with someone who's often passive-aggressive, encouraging that person to establish and defend her or his boundaries can help end the destructive cycle. Most important, you need to be particularly vigilant about *your own* boundaries, or you may suffer the consequences of their passive-aggression. Because your boundaries and theirs are so intertwined, I will discuss both together here.

Establishing Healthy Boundaries

We have learned that boundaries are usually related to our physical selves, our ego, and our self-image. If you ask people to write down their boundaries, they might stare at you with a wrinkled forehead. Boundaries are often so well established that people don't think of them as rules; they're just "the way I am." For people involved in a relationship where passive-aggression is the third party, however, being explicit about boundaries is essential.

People who behave passive-aggressively may not have boundaries—in fact, the whole notion may seem strange. However, they need to establish such boundaries or they will never step out of the cycle. They should also know your boundaries: a set of guidelines that will tell them exactly what is likely to make you angry or hurt. More important, perhaps, you need to know your boundaries, because it's easy to lose sight of them in this kind of relationship.

Here are some other important qualities of healthy boundaries:

- *Clarity.* You are clear in your own mind where you end and others begin, and those who know you are equally clear.
- *Protection.* Your boundaries make you feel safe. You understand that you are in control of how close others get to you, and they know what lines they should not cross.
- *Flexibility.* You're confident enough to change your boundaries and limits when you feel the situation calls for it, giving you a sense of freedom. You don't build walls to shut people out.

Setting clear, flexible, protective boundaries is essential to healthy identity and self-esteem and to communicating your needs assertively. Developing and asserting your boundaries, even if the experience is uncomfortable at first, will begin to bring the cycle of passive-aggressive behavior to a conclusion.

Exercise: Setting Physical Boundaries

You may work on this exercise alone or with your partner. If you are in a relationship, it would be useful to exchange lists once you've completed them.

1. Find a place where you can be quiet for a half hour or so.
2. Using pen and paper or your favorite digital device, make a list of your boundaries, using this checklist:

- What kind of physical proximity is comfortable for me? With friends or family? With coworkers? With strangers?
- What kind of touching is acceptable? With friends or family? With coworkers? With strangers?
- What kind of barrier do I want around my possessions and personal spaces? Under lock and key? Only touch what you can see? Available with permission? What's mine is yours?
- How do I feel about sexual intimacy? You'll have to wait a while? Only after an emotional relationship is established? I need to feel trust? Whenever you're ready, I'm available?

3. What other physical boundary issues come up for you as you do this exercise? If there are particular concerns in your relationship, raise them here. For example, you might want your partner to use a gentler tone of voice when you are discussing problems.
4. Sit with your list for a few minutes. Does this honestly reflect your boundaries? If you've had trouble setting boundaries, consider what might make you feel more comfortable.

Although physical boundaries may be the easiest to identify and accept, people who have been stuck in a passive-aggressive loop may still have problems with both parts. They may not be used to thinking of themselves as *having* boundaries. Reviewing this chapter and the list their partner develops may help them to consider not what their boundaries *should* be, but what boundaries might make them feel safer and more comfortable in the world.

The partners of those in such relationships should be wary of complaints that they are being rigid or unreasonable or inflexible. Examine your boundaries, of course, but trust yourself on this.

Exercise: Setting Emotional Boundaries

Again, you may work on this exercise alone or with your partner.

1. Find a place where you can be quiet for a half hour or so.

2. Using pen and paper or your favorite digital device, make a list of recent issues in your relationship.

    - When was the last time you felt angry because of something your partner said or did? What happened?
    - When was the last time you were hurt by something your partner said or did? What happened?
    - If you could change one thing about your partner's behavior, what would it be?
    - If there were one thing that could make you happier in your relationship, what would it be?

3. Review your list. Can you think of a boundary that would have prevented your being angry or hurt?

4. Using the list, develop some emotional boundaries that you think might enhance your relationship. For example, if you would like to change your partner's habit of taking your pens and not returning them, you might write, "My personal things belong to me. You should ask before you borrow and always return what you take."

5. Sit with your list for a few minutes. Do you feel comfortable with what you've written?

Because these issues are close to the heart of the relationship, you may need to consider the sharing process carefully. It might be best to "trade" with your partner one item at a time. Be wary if those who are stuck in a passive-aggressive loop quickly agree to everything you say. Watch their behavior; it will tell you much more about their actual willingness to respect your boundaries and meet your needs.

Advice for Partners

If your partner is truly committed to leaving the passive-aggressive cycle behind, the mutual exercises in the last section may help to set you on the road, particularly in conjunction with the communication strategies in Key 5. This is not always the case, however. Let's look in again on Karen and Ray.

> *The six months that followed Karen's threat to leave—and Ray's begging her to stay—were a rocky road. Karen told Ray that things would have to change, and the simplest place to start seemed to be with the way the place was furnished. When she moved in, Ray had suggested she sell her "old furniture"— which, she had to admit, was older than his and a little shabby. Now she wanted to make some changes.*
>
> *First, she bought new drapes for the living room. They were green, and Ray said he didn't like green. The second set were striped. Ray wrinkled his nose. Finally she got a set of pale tan drapes that more or less matched the walls. They pleased Ray, but she felt she hadn't made much of a dent.*
>
> *She bought a new set of dishes, and she unpacked some kitchen things she especially loved, including a beer mug from Munich's Oktoberfest and a teacup that had been her grandmother's. Within a week or two, both of them had turned up broken. Ray said it was surely the cleaning woman, but Karen wondered.*
>
> *A couple of times, she tried to sit Ray down and talk things over. Usually, the conversation was very short. Ray would become upset. She didn't love him, he would say; she was going to leave. Her trying to comfort him always turned into sex.*

Tolerance for passive-aggressive behavior varies from person to person, and it may also depend on the positive characteristics the person is bringing to your relationship. Understand, however, that you may reach a place, like Karen, where ordinary steps are not enough to make you comfortable in the relationship.

How to Help Your Partner

Passive-aggression means that partners have difficulty setting their own boundaries, so you need to be especially firm about enforcing your own. This means converting your boundaries into *explicit limits* on their behavior. Yes, this sounds like police tactics, and in some respects, a police officer is what you'll become.

- Establish your boundaries clearly; they will be your guide in establishing the other person's *limits*.
- Be clear about what you want and what your partner can and can't do, and explain that you want more than her or his promise of compliance; you want performance.
- Be prepared to enforce these limits without exception. Flexibility will only confuse a person with a passive-aggressive personality. Your goal here is to safeguard your own boundaries. A happy side effect might be the ability to model to your partner how to step outside the passive-aggressive loop.
- Communicate your displeasure. For instance, Karen might say, "When you come home late to avoid meeting my friends, I feel that you're treating them and me with disrespect. If you care about me, then knowing my friends should matter to you."

Setting limits lets partners know that you understand that they are not giving you the treatment you deserve. Be specific about what bothers you, specific about your expectations, clear about your intent and willingness to help them. Try to follow the biblical rule: Hate the sin, not the sinner. In Ray's case, he's not rude. His behavior is.

Also, wait to have this conversation until you have understood and released your own anger. Partners should feel that you are setting limits in an effort to make your relationship work, not to punish them. You're telling them what to do or avoid doing if they also want to be with you.

Setting limits sounds easy in theory, but in practice, people who are stuck in a passive-aggressive loop will put up a fight using their familiar tools.

Karen invited some friends for dinner on a Friday night, and she made it clear to Ray that she wanted him there. On time. No excuses. He was home early, and he dressed appro-

priately. During dinner, however, he didn't seem to be engaged in the conversation. When the meal was over, he excused himself to make a phone call and was gone for 10 minutes. After her friends left, Karen took a deep breath and expressed her disappointment.

"It was nice to have you here with me, but you seemed distracted."

"Did I?" Ray asked innocently. "Why do you say that?"

"Well, you hardly said anything to our guests, for one thing. Sometimes I wondered if you were paying attention at all."

Ray shook his head. "You know how work is. I'm sorry, but I suppose I was thinking about that call I had to make."

"Did you listen to anything we were saying?" Karen was getting angry again.

"Well, actually, I did. You know they weren't talking about anything that interests me. You really seemed to enjoy their company though, so it wasn't a waste."

How to Help Yourself

If you are partnered with someone attached to passive-aggressive behavior, it's most important to take care of yourself. You can set limits, but people with passive-aggression are highly skilled at making excuses or slipping away from doing what you ask. While you can hold partners accountable, you cannot control their behavior. You can only control your own.

It's important to have your own boundaries clear in your mind so that you understand when they are being crossed. It is not your job—in fact, it is not in your power—to rescue the person with passive-aggressiveness. You can make excuses for her or him and try to delay the consequences of the person's behavior, but in the end, you will only hurt yourself.

At least with yourself, you must insist on honest and open communication. When partners lie or make excuses, you need to honor your assessment. Tell them that you see the truth of what they are feeling from what they are doing. At least for yourself, unravel the ambiguity of your partners' behavior: What can you expect from them? Finally, and most important, you need to be clear about how you feel and how far you can go in your relationships without suffering too many wounds.

> Karen was offered a job that would take her to a city more than 1,000 miles from where she lived with Ray. Her first reaction was excitement: It was a great opportunity and a chance to make a fresh start. When she thought about leaving Ray, she found that the prospect wasn't entirely unpleasant. It felt a lot like relief. When he came home that evening, she told him her news.
>
> "I've been offered a job in Kansas City, and I think I'm going to take it," she said.
>
> He looked stunned. "You would leave me?"
>
> "Well, frankly, I don't think our relationship is going anywhere. By now, I thought we might be engaged, but I'm not happy the way we are."
>
> "You never said you wanted to get married!" A little anger was showing now.
>
> "Actually, that's not what I want, not the way you are now."
>
> "Well, do whatever you want to do," he said, leaving the room.
>
> She did. She left.

I'm not urging you to abandon a passive-aggressive relationship at the first signs of trouble. As you will find in this book, there are a number of strategies you can use to reduce the passive-aggressive behavior and relate to your partner in more open and intimate ways. You need to at least consider setting some time limits, however, or years down the road you could find yourself still hearing promises and excuses instead of seeing changed behavior and a stronger relationship. If you are as far down that road as Karen finds herself, it may be time to consider walking away, or at least taking a time-out to see how your feelings change when you have some emotional distance.

Keep in mind that—regardless of whether passive-aggression is an issue—some things remain true:

- People are responsible for how they feel, even if they choose to deny those feelings.
- People have to own the choices they make, good and bad.
- People need to understand and communicate their needs and boundaries in order to build a sound relationship.

Woven through this chapter is the need for honest and compassionate communication between people, rather than exchanges that evade feelings and excuse behavior. In the next chapter, we look at assertive communication and how it can contribute to breaking the passive-aggressive cycle and healing damaged relationships.

COMMUNICATE ASSERTIVELY

Abby and Jim were traveling in England with some friends when Abby stumbled on the cobblestones. She put out an arm to break her fall and instead broke her arm—just a hairline fracture, but enough to put her in a local emergency room for the afternoon while the others looked at some of the ancient colleges.

Jim stayed with her in the hospital and held her hand, but he was quiet. He was thinking about last year's trip to Italy. That time, Abby missed the last step coming out of a church and fell hard on her knees. Nothing was broken, but one knee was badly bruised. The traveling group—some of Jim's old friends from college—was headed for the Lake Country. They would be sleeping in a different place every night, and day hikes were planned. Jim knew they couldn't keep up, so he and Abby stayed in Venice for several days and caught up with the group in Milan.

As they waited now in the Oxford hospital, Abby was upset. "I'm so sorry," Abby said again and again. Jim just nodded and tried to smile. Finally, she added, "I'm just so clumsy at times." He laughed. "Yeah, especially when we travel." She laughed with him, but it didn't feel funny. Actually, she had forgotten about the time in Venice, but when she thought about it, she remembered those few days as one of the best vacations ever—she had rarely felt as close to Jim as she did then. Abby was Jim's second wife—quite a bit younger than him—and the friends they traveled with were his college

*buddies and their wives. She knew he liked to spend time
with them, but she had been happy to be alone with him for
a while.*

*This time it was only Abby's arm that was broken. As Jim
said when they rejoined the group for dinner, "At least this
time, we can stay on the road with you guys. Unless we have
to walk on our hands—then I'll rethink it." The men teased
Jim about looking for an excuse to hole up with Abby at a
country inn in the Cotswolds, and the women were very sym-
pathetic. Abby wondered what Jim was thinking, but she figured the whole episode would blow over. After all, the cobblestones were wet—it's not like she had fallen on purpose.*

*Still, he spent a lot of time walking with his college friends,
busy taking pictures, leaving her behind with the wives. With
her cast, some things were more difficult for her to do, but the
wives helped her—and they were so thoughtful that it made
her feel special.*

At this point in the book, you may recognize some of the
passive-aggressive behavior that's in play here. Jim is making
jokes about his wife's injury, but they seem quite pointed and
not designed to make her feel better. And with two injuries on
two consecutive trips, we have to wonder a little bit about Abby's
behavior.

What's clear is that the communication lines between the two
are down. If boundaries are the map of our self-image, then the
lines are drawn with words. In Key 4, we saw that boundaries are
a crucial issue in passive-aggressive relationships. To let people
know where our boundaries lie, we need to engage in effective
communication.

Both steps become a challenge when passive-aggressiveness
enters the picture. People in the passive-aggressive loop often
have no boundaries, or their boundaries are blurred; their partners have to define and guard their own boundaries carefully or
they may be overrun. In addition, people with a passive-aggressive
behavior style are reluctant to tell others about their boundaries
because they fear that to do so will involve anger—either in them-

selves, and showing anger is something they greatly fear, or in their partners, and they don't want to risk losing them.

If you have spent years being afraid to express your needs openly, then it may be hard for you to say what you're feeling or to tell others what you want at the risk of disappointing or angering them. The goal of this key is to help you to move beyond passive-aggressive behavior—or at least to take a few small steps toward more honest and direct communication. If you're trying to stop your own passive-aggression, you will discover ways to begin clearly communicating your needs without fearing conflict. For partners, this key will help you to develop clear, positive ways of communicating with the person who exhibits passive-aggression. You will learn strategies for communicating in a productive way that won't spark their defensive behavior.

Both of you must understand what assertive communication looks like. You must also understand that if people disagree assertively—with good intentions and mutual respect—their exchange can help to build a stronger, more intimate relationship. Let's begin by looking at the four primary communication styles—assertive, aggressive, passive, and passive-aggressive—so that you can see which most closely matches your style.

Communication Styles

In the introduction, we looked at the four personality styles. Here we want to go back to them and focus on the kinds of communication they involve.

Aggressive Communication

Plagued by low self-esteem and a sense of powerlessness, those who engage in aggressive behavior tend to bluster and bully their way through conversation. This may express itself as rage, screaming, or insults, but *loud* isn't the whole story. The goal of aggressive communication is domination, and the skilled player may be able to do this with jokes or stories or expertise. The biggest clue is that no one else gets to talk. The aggressive communicator's basic message is, "You have nothing to say about this!"

Aggressive communicators are:

- *Reactive and threatening.* They "snap" easily, storming into and out of rooms, and escalating to rage when someone disagrees with them. Their posture, tone of voice, and words are intended to intimidate.
- *Critical and blaming.* When something has gone wrong, they attack, blame, and denigrate.
- *Overbearing.* They speak loudly and interrupt often in order to "be heard."
- *Domineering.* Winning is everything. They won't quit until the other person gives up.

Passive Communication

People who communicate passively rarely say much, and they certainly avoid expressing their needs, standing up for their rights, and speaking their minds. Passive individuals often ignore insults, grievances, and violations of their boundaries. If they occasionally erupt with resentment or anger, they are immediately embarrassed by their outburst and retreat into passivity. The passive communicator's message is, "It's okay."

Passive communicators are:

- *Apologetic.* They say "sorry" after expressing even the smallest need and make excuses for other people who treat them poorly.
- *Retiring.* Their body language is tentative; they make poor eye contact and speak timidly.
- *Confused.* Ask them for an opinion, and they'll fumble for words until someone picks up the conversational ball.
- *People pleasing.* It's hard to make a mutual decision with passive communicators. To the question, "What do you want?" they reply, "Whatever you want."

Passive-Aggressive Communication

On the surface, passive-aggressive communication may look the same as passive communication, but you need to listen more closely. While the passive communicator may explode on rare occasion, the anger of a passive-aggressive communicator is more likely to slip out in criticism and sarcasm. The passive-aggressive communicator may be unaware of the impact her or his statements make—or at least may seem unaware. The passive-aggressive message might be, "I don't know why you're upset; I didn't mean anything."

Passive-aggressive communicators are:

- *Mutterers.* They speak so softly they can't be heard, or they mutter under their breath. If you ask, they said "nothing."
- *Double messages.* While their words say one thing, their expression says something else. The face is smiling, but the words sound mean.
- *Sarcastic.* They hide behind sarcasm. If you say you don't want to go out, they'll respond, "You must be so tired." Their tone conveys anything but sympathy.

Assertive Communication

Arising from a strong sense of self-worth and the desire to positively establish boundaries, needs, and rights, assertive communication is direct and clear. In this style, people also want to listen, and they have empathy for the other person or people in the conversation. Assertive communication is constructive and collaborative, looking for ways to achieve a situation where both people are happy.

Assertive communicators are:

- *Nonreactive and respectful.* They don't respond to anger with anger; instead, they state their needs and feelings clearly.
- *Confident but collaborative.* They stand up for themselves, but they also want to have a true meeting of minds.

- *Good listeners.* They appreciate that other people may have different opinions, and they want to listen.
- *Control.* They make eye contact, have a relaxed posture, and speak with a calm voice.

Assertive communication enriches relationships, helps people understand each other better, and engenders closeness and intimacy.

Why Assertive Communication Works

Assertive communication is an effective way of expressing how you feel at the same time that you learn how the other person is feeling about the same situation. If you and your partner have succeeded in communicating assertively, you should both feel good about the exchange and its outcome. Let's go back and see how the planning for Abby and Jim's trip took place.

After dinner one night, Jim announced plans for a trip to England. "I heard from Paul today. We've been sending e-mails back and forth about this year's group vacation. Looks like it's going to be England."

"Oh," Abby said, feeling a rush of disappointment. "Is there a group trip every year?"

"Most years—we've been doing it ever since we graduated. Otherwise, I'd never see those guys. Anyway, you and the wives get to go along—you liked them, right?"

"Yes, they're very nice."

Jim sensed Abby wasn't happy. "What's the matter? You don't like England? You've been there already?"

"No, no, England will be great," Abby said, mustering some enthusiasm. "It's over 10 years since I was there last. I'm sure you'll have fun."

"Good," Jim said. "I'll have the wives get in touch with you about dates and stuff." He reached for the remote control.

This conversation takes a wrong turn almost immediately. First, Jim is the aggressor in this case. He's delivering a decision, not inviting a conversation. And instead of expressing her surprise, Abby hides her distress and begins to acquiesce. Let's see how it might have gone if Abby had changed her response.

> After dinner one night, Jim announced plans for a trip to England. "I heard from Paul today. We've been sending e-mails back and forth about this year's group vacation. Looks like it's going to be England."
>
> "Oh," Abby said, feeling a rush of disappointment. "I thought we might go somewhere on our own this year. We had such a good time in Venice."
>
> Jim smiled. "Venice was great. But the four of us always do a group trip with our wives—it's our only way to stay in touch."
>
> Abby nodded. "Staying close to old friends is important. I know they're important to you, and I like them."
>
> Jim noticed her hesitation. "But?"
>
> "We're both so busy with our work that we don't have a lot of time to be together without distractions. Maybe we need to get away to do that."
>
> "Venice was nice, even with your banged-up knee," Jim said, "but I don't know if we can afford two big trips this year."
>
> "It wouldn't have to be a big trip. We could just go to the mountains for a long weekend."
>
> "I've heard of a place, actually. I'll look into it."
>
> "England will be fun," Abby said, feeling some real excitement now. "Have you guys done the itinerary yet?"

Notice that both sides are being sensitive to each other in this conversation. They're clearly expressing their own desires, but they're listening to each other's needs, too. And although they both have different needs, there's nothing here that you could call quarrelling. The differences are expressed with respect, calmness, and clarity.

One reason that people caught in the passive-aggressive loop have so much trouble with conflict is that they see it only one way:

"If we don't agree, we will get angry. We'll start yelling at each other. There will be hurt feelings, and one of us will end up losing." That's usually the passive-aggressive person. Avoiding that pain or conflict becomes all important, so people passive-aggressively bottle up their anger and express it in covert, indirect ways.

But this is not the inevitable result of conflict. In fact, research has shown that conflict—even if it's occasionally uncomfortable—can help to create good, enriching relationships. We'll be taking a closer look at conflict in Key 6, but before we leave the topic, here's another possible conversation between Abby and Jim, one where the conflict has a little more edge.

> *After dinner one night, Jim announced plans for a trip to England. "I heard from Paul today. We've been sending e-mails back and forth about this year's group vacation. Looks like it's going to be England."*
>
> *"Ah," she said. "I didn't realize that a group trip was being planned again."*
>
> *"Sure," Jim said. "I guess I didn't mention it before. The guys usually pick the place—the wives seem to be happy enough to go along."*
>
> *Abby felt her anger rising. Jim's three college friends were still married to "first wives," and they were smart, interesting women, but they were always referred to as a collective. "That's an interesting expression, 'the wives,'" she said, searching for a way to describe her feelings. "I think of them as Sally, Chris, and Pam."*
>
> *"Yes?" Jim could tell that more was coming.*
>
> *"I know I'm the new wife. Are the others just getting the news tonight, too?"*
>
> *Jim was feeling uncomfortable. "Are you upset?"*
>
> *"I'm thinking that half the fun of a trip is anticipation. If you guys want to make the decision, that's okay, but it would be nice to know what you're considering. Sally, Chris, Pam, and I might have some useful information for you as you're figuring out what you want to do."*
>
> *Jim was irritated; his first wife had never fussed about*

things like this, but then she was nothing like Abby. "Is that important to you?"

Abby beamed. "Thank you for asking. Yes, it is kind of important."

"Okay, then." He thought a minute. "You know, we picked England, but we haven't worked out the details. Maybe the wives—" He saw her wince. "Maybe Sally, Chris, Pam, and you might want to come up with some ideas."

She smiled.

"That's better then?" he asked.

"Much. I'll call them."

At the end of this conversation, Jim has learned that his new wife wants more of a role in the decisions that affect both of them. She hasn't made an explicit point of it, but she's also been talking about having more respect for women. One of the things I try to help couples understand is that conflict can strengthen relationships if it's carried out in the right way. Constructive conflict is assertive communication in action.

People who are caught in a passive-aggressive cycle need to reconsider conflict and understand that its outcome depends on the style of the conversation it starts.

Principles of Assertive Communication

Assertive communication has certain characteristics regardless of the people involved or the topics being discussed: using empathy, *I* messages, active listening, and validating statements. Let's look at each of these.

Look Out for Both of You

One building block of assertive communication—and the broadest—may seem counterintuitive. I know I've been telling you that you need to express your needs and your boundaries clearly. At the same time, you need to keep in mind the needs and boundaries of the other person. Abby may want to go back to Venice for a week alone with Jim, but she recognizes—and respects—his need to spend some time attending to old friendships. Jim, in turn, feels that she's crossing boundaries his previous wife never threatened, but he appreciates that she's a different person.

The best assertive communications result in a win-win outcome. Some experts in this area believe that *not losing* is more important than *winning*. People don't want to feel that they've been ripped off or that their wants and feelings have been disregarded. By taking a win-win approach, both partners finish with their power and dignity intact.

Although it may seem to be a word that belongs on another continent in another century, *dignity* is still important to people. Whatever else you lose in a win-lose situation, you also lose your self-respect. For people stuck in a passive-aggressive loop, loss of self-respect can underscore low self-esteem and victimhood. For their partners, it is crucial to retain dignity in a situation that may often feel confusing and breed anger.

So how can you approach communication with the other person's needs and boundaries in mind? Try a little empathy, that quality we discussed briefly in Key 2. Empathy doesn't always come easily to people who are entrenched in passive-aggressiveness, and it can present some risks to their partners, but it is nevertheless the foundation of assertive conversation.

The classic metaphor for empathy is "putting yourself in someone else's shoes." More to the point is putting yourself in someone else's skin: feeling what they feel and seeing yourself and the world from their point of view. Empathy adds depth to the love we feel for family, partners, and friends. We see them for who they are, not who we imagine them to be. We appreciate them for their qualities, not just what they do for us, and we acknowledge that they may have different thoughts and feelings, even when they're sharing the same experience with us. Feeling empathy, we try to support *their* needs, not just what we would want in the situation.

"The Gift of the Magi," a widely read short story by O. Henry, provides a great example. A couple had very little money, but they wanted to give each other the perfect Christmas gift. He sells his watch so that he can buy some beautiful combs and ornaments for her long, lustrous hair. She sells her hair to buy a fob for his watch. Although we may hope for a better outcome, we feel empathy when we support what our loved one wants and needs, rather than responding to what we would want in the same situation.

Without empathy, you may assume that another family member's needs and boundaries are the same as yours and that they are experiencing life as you do. This view ignores their individuality, and as a result, you can make assumptions that get you into trouble. You may feel offended when you take someone to a sushi bar you love, only to find out that he will never eat raw food. If you see someone in terms of what she or he has always provided for you— for example, being a companion for the theater—you may be upset when that person no longer wants to go.

Besides honoring their individuality, you need to understand people at a deep level in order to treat them with empathy. Empathy gives other people the message that you "get" them—and we all want to be "gotten," especially by those closest to us. Building empathy can help you over the hurdles of a passive-aggressive behavior pattern and connect you more intimately to the people you love.

Besides soothing your loved ones, empathy is good for your health, too, according to research. Regularly meditating, or thinking, about the well-being of others has been shown to reduce the inflammatory response your body has to stress and decrease your risk of related health issues, including heart disease, diabetes, and dementia.

Exercise: Learning Empathy

1. Think about your partner, friend, family member, or coworker.
2. What has her or his mood been like in recent days?
3. What's going on in this person's life that might be making her or him happy or sad, anxious or angry?
4. How are you contributing?
5. What could you do or say to improve this person's situation?

Developing empathy is a crucial lesson for people stuck in a passive-aggressive loop. Their partners need to watch and make sure that empathy doesn't slide into a pattern of making excuses for the other person's behavior.

Speak for Yourself

When we treat each other with empathy, we are attempting to see the world—or the immediate situation—from another's point of view. This is different, however, from assuming that we know what someone else is thinking and feeling. Part of empathy—an essential part—is seeing others as individuals.

In assertive communication, we reflect this understanding by using "I" statements. That is, we tell people what we think or feel, we don't accuse them of causing the problem, and we don't tell them what they must do to fix it.

ASSERTIVE: "*I'm* tired today and would be happy for some help."

PASSIVE-AGGRESSIVE: "If *you* can spare the time, *you* could help me with this. *You* never get involved in household chores."

The use of *you* is often an effort to control or criticize, and it doesn't always have to be mean-spirited. To the hearer, however, *even well-intentioned criticism can bite. The best criticism is requested before it's offered.* Here are some examples that show how "I" statements can change the impact of a statement, even if it has negative content.

"You" Statement (*Accusatory*)	"I" Statement (*Nonjudgmental*)
"You really hurt my feelings when you criticized my cooking in front of everyone."	"I felt embarrassed and angry to hear that you didn't like the dinner I made for our friends. I want to know what you think, but I would rather hear it privately."

"You should get to the dentist to do something about your teeth. They're really yellow."

"I was reading the other day about this new whitening treatment for teeth. Have you heard about it?"

"You made a mess of this job. You just don't get what we're doing here."

"I'd like to sit down with you and talk about your last assignment. I want to explain how it connects with our overall strategy."

"Why don't you ever say what you mean? You're driving me crazy."

"I feel that you're holding something back. I would prefer to hear what you're really thinking, even if it means we disagree."

Passive-aggressive communication assumes that all discussion will lead to a quarrel. This example shows how criticism can be communicated in nonthreatening ways. It also provides an important lesson for partners who worry that the least little complaint they make will upset their passive-aggressive friend. "I" statements tend to diffuse defensiveness and help people to open up about actions or statements that have evoked anger or pain in their partners.

Listen to Learn

If you've ever been in a group discussion, you may have noticed this. Someone is so eager to be heard that she's not following the flow of the conversation. While she's rehearsing her statement—in her head—the conversation drifts in an entirely different direction. Once she gets to speak, she's really off point. Or she may say the same thing someone else said while she was lost in her own thoughts.

This happens in two-sided conversations as well. *Hearing* is a passive activity. Our ears are biologically open, and sound waves pass through to register on nerve endings in the inner ear. *Listening* is much more active and holistic. Besides the ears, it engages the thinking brain, memories, and feelings. Listening and empathy are good partners for a chicken-or-egg argument. You can grow empathy by listening, and empathy will help you become a better listener. Here's how effective listening works.

- *Be in the moment.* Clear your mind of any concerns you've had that don't relate to the present conversation, and quiet any upsetting reactions you've had to an initial statement.
- *Put aside your ego-based defenses.* If anger or other emotions are too powerful—either in yourself or your partner—suggest a postponed conversation. Don't retaliate or "disappear" if you hear something negative from your partner.
- *Think and feel positive.* Get in touch with the compassion and empathy you have for your partner, and understand that his intentions are positive and his feelings for you sound.
- *Keep your eye on the prize.* As you listen, look for points where you agree—or are very close to agreeing—and try to build on those.

Childhood experiences have told people in a passive-aggressive loop that no one is listening to them. Partners who develop excellent listening skills can make a powerful impact in helping them to feel safe and respected.

Confirm Your Partner's Feelings

Another strategy for helping people with passive-aggression is to confirm their feelings. This proves that you've listened, you've gotten the message, and you can read it back to them so you're both on the same page. In therapy, I've often seen patients who have this hunger to be heard and understood. When their family doesn't acknowledge them, they build a reservoir of anger over time, and we've seen how this contributes to passive-aggressiveness. In the heading for this section, I purposely avoided the buzzword *validation*, but that is what I mean. I just want to be clear about its meaning.

When we go to a movie with a friend, one of the first things we ask when the lights go up is, "What did you think?" For most of us, this is a simple sharing of opinion. Our self-esteem isn't involved in the response, and in fact, we may enjoy a bit of back and forth about what we liked and didn't like, who performed best, and so on.

True validation takes place at a deeper level. As children's experiences become wider and more complicated, parents should help them to understand their feelings and accept them. We've seen, however, that many parents overlook this job or botch it up because of their own fear of feelings. This is one of the childhood patterns that can grow into passive-aggressiveness. Partners can help those with passive-aggression to repair this old wound, and validation through assertive communication is a good strategy.

1. *Reflect back what your partner says.* To make sure that you are clearly understanding your partner, repeat the information back *without adding information of your own.* You'll need to listen closely. Sometimes you may need to go back and forth more than once before you can get everything straight.

   SUE: The boss is holding a seminar on the new computer project, and so far I haven't gotten an invitation.
   BILL: So they're holding a seminar and you want to go, but you haven't been invited. Is that it?
   SUE: Yes.
   BILL: But I sense that there's more. Is the seminar important for your job?
   SUE: I know quite a bit about computers, but the seminar

might help me do my job better. If everyone else is going and I'm not, what does it say about my position?

BILL: You're feeling left out, and you're worried about the impact this might have on your job.

2. *Validate your partner's feelings.* Let your partner know that you understand.

> **BILL:** I would be upset, too, in that situation. You work hard at that job, and you deserve respect.
>
> **SUE:** Thanks; I think so, too. I don't know why I'm being snubbed.

3. *Express empathy.* Let your partner know you have had similar feelings.

> **BILL:** I had the same experience once. I was left out of a trip that just about everybody was making to the Phoenix branch. I stewed quite a bit before the boss explained that she needed someone she trusted in the home office while they were away.
>
> **SUE:** So maybe I'm not being snubbed.
>
> **BILL:** It might be worth finding out.

In typical passive-aggressive style, Sue had avoided talking to her boss about the invitation, sure that it meant an insult and maybe even a potential threat to her job. Her partner, Bill, was able to help her express her feelings and explore their possible meanings. His reassurance gave her the courage to take the subject up with her boss. As it turned out, Sue's boss had felt that the seminar was too basic for her level of expertise. He said she was more than welcome to attend—she might even be able to add something; he just didn't want to waste her time with something she didn't need.

Making a Start

Reading this chapter, you've learned a lot about assertive communication and how it can help you escape the passive-aggressive loop you've been running in, probably since childhood. The examples have shown how you can express your anger in positive ways, using the message it tells you to identify unmet needs and violated boundaries. Then you can get what you want without angry words, accusations, sarcasm, and manipulation.

- Practice saying no to requests. If you don't have the time, say so clearly and concisely. Explanations are not required.
- Start using "I" statements to express your dissatisfaction with the situation. "I don't think that's fair" is much less inflammatory than "You're trying to cheat me."
- Become aware of your body language when dealing with a potential conflict. Make eye contact, stand firm (no shuffling from foot to foot), and don't make dramatic gestures.
- Become conscious of your emotional reactions and how they feel in your body. Work on keeping them out of the discussion. You need to feel your emotions, but then turn to reasoned words to express your concern.
- Practice assertive communication in low-risk environments, such as with friends and coworkers. Don't ask your hard-nosed boss for a big raise on the first day.

Advice for Partners

If you're living or working with a person who engages in passive-aggressive behavior, you know that trying to address it can be like walking through a minefield. Say the wrong thing, and you may run into a wall of defensiveness and denial. In passive-aggression, people don't want to deal with their anger directly or face the consequences of their covert actions. They can stonewall you or even throw your accusations right back in your face. It's enough to make *you* explode, however, and that gets you nowhere as a couple.

How You Can Help Your Partner

Over the years, people with passive-aggression have learned that it's safest to conceal their anger, jealousy, fear, resentment, and hurt feelings. In a good relationship, however, you may persuade them to talk about what's going on inside. They have to develop the trust that you won't retaliate against them or label them as "wrong." You have to find a way to make both of you feel heard and respected. You need to communicate assertively in your own right—clearly, fairly, and unemotionally—with the goal of meeting both your needs and theirs.

People with passive-aggressiveness can learn to be more direct if you follow the guidelines for assertive communication in this chapter: seeing their side of the issue, listening to what they have to say (quietly and respectfully, even if you don't like what they are saying), and validating their responses. You may realize that an open discussion can be positive, but they don't; you have to ease information out of them.

I remember vividly the way my mother-in-law used to withdraw when she was upset. It was like clear plastic came down around her; you could see her, but you definitely couldn't reach her. In the early years of our marriage, my husband would do the same thing. I'd think, "You've turned into Margaret!" (By the way, never tell someone they're acting like one of their parents. It's sure to start a fight!) Instead, I said, "When it appears that you're stonewalling me—when I can see you, but you're not really there—I get really frustrated. I need you to be present and respond to me."

A patient recently complained that her husband had come home irritable and grumpy. I said, "Did you ask him what was going on?" She said, "No, I just told him he was being irritable and grumpy." I find that, very often, people just don't ask each other about what they think or how they're feeling. Why don't they? In part, the reason is the emotion-phobia so many people feel. If they haven't done the personal work of clearing up issues from the past, they're afraid another's display of feelings will spark their own. They don't want to hear what's going on with someone else, in case it hurts their feelings or makes them angry.

When you see your partner pulling away instead of sharing, gently say, "I sense that you're a little withdrawn. I wonder if something's going on with you. I'd be happy to listen if you need to talk." Or, "If you feel like talking about it, I'm here." Be sure to use soft language like "I sense" and "you *seem*" rather than "you *are*," which could be perceived as accusatory, critical, or presumptuous. If you're wrong, you might upset the other person when nothing was wrong in the first place!

Let's check in with Abby and Jim one more time to see how their time in the emergency room might have been spent more productively. In this case, let's assume that Abby is the passive-aggressive personality and Jim has fallen into some passive-aggressive habits as a result of their connection.

> As they waited now in the Oxford hospital, Abby was upset. "I'm so sorry," she said again and again.
>
> "I'm sorry, too," Jim said. "The trip is more fun when you're able to participate."
>
> Reassured that he didn't seem angry with her, Abby said, "You're remembering when I hurt my knee in Venice."
>
> He squeezed her hand. "Actually, I was. This is two trips in a row when you've been injured."
>
> "I know I spoiled the Italy trip for you, but I'm not trying to get hurt, you know."
>
> Feeling her bristle, he put an arm around her shoulder. "Of course not, and you didn't spoil the trip. It was just different. We had a great time in Venice, don't you think?"
>
> She settled down. "It was a great time, but you were supposed to be off hiking with your friends. I'm really sorry. This time, that won't happen."

Jim nodded. "We can spend an extra day here because I'd like to visit the colleges. We'll catch up with the others in London. It will be fine."

"You're not angry?"

"I was at first, but mostly I'm concerned. We know you have issues with passive-aggressiveness, and I want to be sure that you can tell me if you're upset about something so that we can work it out."

People who have developed passive-aggressive behavior have trouble talking about feelings for fear that they'll start a conflict or gradually lose your attention. Partners may need to initiate the conversation—lacing it, as Jim did, with reassurances about their affection and their willingness to hear the other person out.

How You Can Help Yourself

Setting some ground rules for communication will give you an enforcement tool to keep your passive-aggressive friends from sliding back into the comfortable (for them) routine of sarcasm, gossip, and guilt. Ground rules are a way to assure them that the discussion will be peaceful, and they build a structure in which you can communicate more easily.

Depending on your relationship, you may have some ideas about ground rules. Here's a place to start:

- When you set a time to talk, both of you are fully engaged. No phones or other distractions.
- No accusations and blaming are allowed. Both of you stick to how you're feeling, without assuming why the other person said or did something you found objectionable.
- Take turns, and no "talking over" what the other person is saying. If necessary, pass an item back and forth that designates you as the speaker.
- No shouting. If someone believes that angry feelings are building toward an explosion, you can take a time-out where neither per-

son talks. If the anger is still hot at the end of that time, postpone your discussion until you both come to the table ready to talk quietly.

These guidelines will give you both a safe place to express your feelings and discuss any issues that have come up between you.

In this chapter, we've seen how assertive communication can help people involved in a passive-aggressive relationship discuss their thoughts and feelings in productive ways. We've also touched upon the importance of demythologizing conflict and making it less scary. Because the fear of conflict plays such a crucial role in the passive-aggressive dance, we'll take up this subject further in Key 6.

REFRAME CONFLICT

M olly lives in the same city as her single son, Daniel. Now divorced, she has a lot of time to herself. She wants to see Daniel, but she thinks if she says that outright, he'll feel sorry for her. Instead, she has invited Daniel to come over for dinner every Friday night. She likes the idea of having something to look forward to at the end of the week, and she figures Daniel, like his father, would never think of cooking for himself. She knows she's not a great cook, but she makes the old-fashioned comfort foods: roasts with gravies, mashed potatoes, and vegetables microwaved in their handy freezer packages. Daniel has always loved her cooking.

To her son, one of the biggest benefits of moving out of his parents' home was getting away from his mother's food. During college, he learned that salads and pastas were tasty alternatives to the protein-heavy meals of his childhood, and he was astonished to learn that even cooked vegetables could be crisp. Since he got his own apartment, he's bought a cookbook or two and started to make his own meals. Daniel likes his mother, and he guesses that she's socially adrift since the divorce, but he hates the food that comes with their visits. Afraid to tell her how he feels, he makes excuses—sometimes at the last minute—that get him out of the requisite meals. Instead of once a week, he visits once a month.

Molly is deeply hurt by his absence. She imagines a variety of reasons why he might not want to come to dinner, most of them involving his preference for her ex-husband or his reluc-

*tance to spend time with her—none of the men in the family
seem to care about her. She has thought of asking him why he
stays away, but she's afraid to hear the answer.*

Like most people, Molly and Daniel are deathly afraid of the
conflict that might result if they openly expressed their needs and
desires. When it comes right down to it, Molly isn't invested in
the meal—she thinks she's offering Daniel a carrot to attract his
presence, unaware that it is ironically the stick driving him away.
Her real need is for his company and his love. Daniel enjoys her
company and cares about her, but he's afraid he'll hurt her feelings if he tells her she's a terrible cook.

There is a better solution, but it involves opening the door to
conflict by expressing their true feelings: Molly wants to see him,
and Daniel doesn't want to eat her cooking. In the case of Molly
and Daniel, the conflict could be so easily resolved.

> *For the third week in a row, Daniel calls on Thursday to
> excuse himself from their family dinner. "I'm sorry, Mom, but
> this business thing came up, and I can't say no."*
>
> *"Your business has kept you away all month," she says.
> "Well, first things first. I'll manage."*
>
> *Daniel hesitates. Then a solution comes to mind. "Look,"
> he says, "Friday is just hard for me. Why don't we make it
> Sunday night, and you come here for a change?"*
>
> *"I suppose I could bring something simple for us to eat,"
> she says, feeling some relief.*
>
> *Daniel winces. "Hey, Mom, I've learned to cook. Just bring
> yourself."*
>
> *Molly is astonished at the delicious meal her son is able to
> deliver. As they talk, she begins to see that Daniel's tastes have
> changed since he was a child. They decide to cook together and
> to alternate Sundays between her house and Daniel's flat.
> They feel a new closeness built around their meals together.*

As you see, conflicts need not involve weapons and blood-
shed, or any resolution that involves winners and losers, injury

and loss. Why the conflict phobia? As with so many things, our attitudes about conflict begin in childhood. If family conflicts involved open expressions of anger—and sometimes violence—our experience tells us that conflict means someone will get hurt—probably us. If we lived in families where conflict was avoided at all cost, we never learned how conflicts can be turned into productive tools that not only resolve disputes but also build understanding and compassion, two keystones of loving relationships. People who rely on passive-aggressive behavior often come from families where models of conflict resolution were lacking. They are also especially eager to avoid conflict because of their great fear that any overt disagreement will lead to the end of their relationships.

Not telling people what we feel because of how they might think or behave is grounded in anxiety that we will be abandoned, left, fired, divorced, or simply cut out of the will, and this produces huge amounts of anger and rage. But expressing our feelings in a compassionate way has no power over anyone, except to the degree people let it have power over them. Although Daniel let his Sunday supper do the talking for him, telling his mother directly that he didn't like her cooking wouldn't kill her. Refusing to go home and join her for a meal cut her to the bone; criticizing her cuisine would be a joy by comparison. Saying you don't like her meatloaf is about you, not about her.

As you can see, I'm suggesting a very different approach to conflict. In the same way that anger is your friend, allowing you to get in touch with your feelings and alerting you to unmet needs and violated boundaries, conflict can also be your ally. When we give in to our fears of anger and conflict, we lock ourselves in a cycle that leaves us unfulfilled and limits or even damages our relationships. This is true for everyone, and while it has special import for those who behave passive-aggressively, it is also sound advice for those important others in their lives.

We all have needs, and these needs sometimes conflict with what others need. It is unrealistic to expect to live without some discord, but beyond that, conflict—when used effectively—can bring us closer to the important people in our lives through greater understanding and a collaborative effort to get everyone's needs met.

So what can you do when needs collide, when you don't see eye to eye with your partner, boss, coworkers, or friends? We explored part of the solution in Key 5: learning how to communicate in ways that are both assertive and compassionate. In Key 6, we take another step, building on communication to learn—step by step—how to handle situations in which we find ourselves at odds with important others in our lives.

Key 6 contains a variety of tried-and-true conflict resolution strategies that will help you arrive at mutually beneficial solutions in all your relationships. These powerful tools show you how to understand the other person's position, share your views effectively, and reach a solution that is better than a compromise. Because all of them are grounded in conversation, let's make a quick review of what we learned in Key 5 as it applies in conflict situations.

Compassionate Assertiveness

Communicating what we want out of life is the only road to achieving our goals and developing the relationships that can support and enrich our lives. Many of us didn't have skilled role models in this part of life; our parents may have inadvertently taught us bad ways to deal with our emotions. This is especially true for those who have developed a passive-aggressive approach to life. It's never too late to learn a different way to communicate that is straightforward about expressing our own position at the same time that it reaches out to others with empathy and compassion.

Passive-aggressiveness is often associated with a posture of helplessness and victimhood, but it is also linked to self-absorption. Compassionate assertiveness speaks to both of those issues.

Expressing ourselves assertively sounds the death knell to victimhood. This style of communication makes us feel powerful and in control, and it also conveys our strength to the people with whom we're interacting. It says, "I believe my thoughts and needs are reasonable, and I am confident that you will want to hear what I have to say."

Listening to others with empathy breaks us out of our self-centered bubble. Beyond their words, we hear the thoughts and needs the other person is trying to convey. We begin to experience the world and our situation from another viewpoint, and it tells important others that we care about them and want to understand them more intimately. It says, "I understand that your thoughts and needs are reasonable, and I respect and care about your well-being."

In the conversations we use to explore and resolve our conflicts with others, compassionate assertiveness is essential. Some unwritten rules will help to make these conversations more fruitful.

Rules of Assertiveness

- Speak calmly; don't rush.
- Be specific; avoid generalizing, as in using words like *always* and *never*.
- Don't assume the other person knows what you're thinking and feeling.
- Present your point of view in a self-assured way.
- Use "I" statements, for example, "I feel a little sad now," not "You hurt my feelings."
- Be conscious of how your voice sounds and what your body language suggests.
- Assertiveness doesn't mean hogging the spotlight or interrupting the other person. Don't.

Rules of Compassion

- Listen with your full attention—no texting, tweeting, or tinkering with games.

- Make frequent eye contact with the other person; don't look away when he or she is speaking.
- Don't show boredom or impatience. If you feel either, adjust your attitude and remind yourself what's really important to you.
- Treat the other person with respect—no mocking or dismissing his or her feelings.
- Ask questions to make sure you understand the other person's point of view.
- Validate what the other person is saying.
- From time to time, repeat back what the other person has told you so that you—and he or she—are clear that you have an understanding of what the person is trying to express. And don't add a negative spin to his or her remarks, for example by saying, "You want to watch that *silly* TV show."

If you practice these communication skills in all of your conversations, they'll be honed and ready to work for you when the talk involves conflict resolution.

General Guidelines to Conflict Resolution

Feeling angry or hurt in the context of a relationship is a clear sign that a conflict is in play. You can begin to resolve that conflict only when you've used the tools in this book to explore your anger or hurt feelings and decide what they're telling you. It is extremely difficult to concentrate on solving a problem when you are enraged or emotionally upset. You can't focus on anything except the inflamed feeling in your body.

The easy thing in such circumstances is to criticize or blame, but that usually triggers defensiveness in your partner. People who have a passive-aggressive approach are particularly sensitive to criticism and are likely to respond automatically with an excuse or defense of their actions or inaction. Instead of playing this loop over and over, you can address the issue itself—instead of the person—and move forward.

The following step-by-step process for conflict resolution can help you avoid the distracting loop and reach a resolution.

Seven Steps to Conflict Resolution

1. Cool down; examine your anger and gain control of your emotions.
2. Discuss and define the problem from each person's point of view.
3. Brainstorm together to come up with ideas and options for solving the problem.
4. Discuss the pros and cons of the various potential solutions.
5. Choose the solution that works best for both parties. Have the intention that everyone wins, or at least no one loses.
6. Execute the solution.
7. Evaluate the solution. Did it work? Meet later to talk about the results. What, if anything, might you do better next time?

This structure will help you deal with disagreements in a way that meets your needs and those of your partner, while enhancing the connection between you. Within this structure, there are some behavioral dos and don'ts that will improve your chances for success. It may be a good idea to make a list of those that seem to apply to your relationship, and you may have others you want to add. Make sure everyone takes a look at the list before you sit down to discuss a problem that has created conflict.

DO	DON'T
• Focus on the present or future.	• Rehash history
• Use a respectful tone of voice	• Raise your voice
• Respect the other person's feelings and ideas	• Criticize, attack, blame, or humiliate
• Take responsibility for your own actions	• Swear at the other person or call him or her names
	• Make insulting facial expressions

DO	DON'T
• Spend the time necessary to reach a resolution • Focus on solving the problem rather than being right	• Tell the other person what to do • Physically attack the other person or threaten violence

Some Useful Strategies

Now that we've got the general framework in hand, here are some specific tools that you might use as you move toward a productive resolution of conflicts. We'll use the case of Sophia and Larry to illustrate.

> *Sophia has been working at home while their son, Paul, has been going through school. Now he's just a year away from high school graduation, and she's restless. She wants to take a job outside the house, but she can't get her husband, Larry, to talk about it. He just shuts down on her. Here's one sample conversation.*
>
> *"I was talking to one of my clients today, and it looks like they may have an opening on staff," Sophia says.*
>
> *"Why do you have to rock the boat? We're happy, aren't we? You've got plenty of work. You have a nice office over the garage. What else can I give you?"*
>
> *"I wish you'd just listen."*
>
> *Larry reaches for the remote control and turns on the news.*

Larry has been dealing with conflict in a passive-aggressive style. If he refuses to talk about the problem, then they're not really arguing, it seems to him. He wants things to stay as they are.

The Taking Turns Conversation

In the Taking Turns Conversation, offered by author and education expert Dr. Marvin Marshall, each person gets a chance to talk while the other person listens. The First Speaker makes a short comment on a topic. The Listener then paraphrases what he or she has just heard, without adding any input. If the First Speaker's message was unclear, the Listener can paraphrase and ask for clarification. The conversation continues, going back and forth in this manner, with the First Speaker as the focus.

After the First Speaker has had the floor for 10 to 15 minutes and the two parties have come to a greater understanding of that person's perspective, the Second Speaker offers thoughts and feelings on the same or a different issue. During the Taking Turns Conversation, the emphasis is on safely exploring current issues.

Sophia persuaded Larry to try using a Taking Turns Conversation to resolve several points of contention.

Using the Taking Turns structure, Sophia explained that while she was making a fairly reliable income doing freelance marketing work at home, there was a cap on how much she could make. She had agreed to work at home while Paul was growing up, but he was a junior in high school now, and extracurricular activities kept him busy—and away from home —until after 5 p.m. She was hearing about job openings with clients she served and thought she might be a good candidate. She was eager to take on a new challenge. Larry listened, and he paraphrased what Sophia told him.

When it was Larry's turn to talk, he shared how worried he had been about having enough money set aside for their son's college years—which were less than two years away. The market ups and downs had cut into what they had already saved, and he was concerned that his own business—he owned and operated a furniture store—was suffering. He told her that he appreciated her willingness to take primary responsibility for Paul during his childhood, but he thought it might be more

sensible for her to delay change until he was safely out of col-
lege and on his own. Sophia listened and summarized Larry's
position.

After a half-hour discussion, Sophia and Larry both felt
the other had made some good points. Sophia said she felt it
was important that they had each listened to the other's per-
spective. She hoped the conversation would help them gener-
ate creative solutions. Larry promised to give problem solving
some serious thought. They agreed to schedule a Win-Win
Solution Brainstorming session for two nights later.

Win-Win Solution Brainstorming, also offered by Dr. Marshall, can take place immediately after a Taking Turns Conversation, or it may be scheduled for a later time.

Win-Win Solution Brainstorming

Maintaining a harmonious relationship means making sure all
parties get what they need to be healthy and happy. Priorities must
sometimes be juggled, but no one should be neglected. If decisions always seem to favor one individual in the household over
everyone else, resentment and bitterness are guaranteed to result.
So, whenever possible, aim for a win-win solution; try to find a way
for all parties to get what they want or need.

This may sound a lot like compromise, but there's a difference.
In a compromise, each person gives up something to arrive at a
solution and, therefore, no one ends up with his or her original
desire. Compromise is necessary sometimes, but win-win solutions are even better.

Win-Win Solution Brainstorming should be employed only after each party understands the feelings and thoughts of the other
regarding a particular issue—after a Taking Turns Conversation,
for example. If you race to solve a problem without understanding
it completely, you are likely to arrive at a solution that will fail
sooner or later. There are eight key steps:

1. *Schedule the* Win-Win Solution Brainstorming *session in advance, if possible.* This way, all parties can give thought to the ideas they'd like to share. Some questions to ask yourself when pondering potential solutions to a problem include:

   - What are my needs and wants in this situation?
   - What does the other party need and want?
   - How can we set up a win-win solution that will serve us both?
   - Will this solution benefit us in the long term, or is it just a temporary fix?
   - Are we both going to be satisfied by this decision, or will one or both of us end up feeling resentful?

2. *Agree to approach the problem as a team, working to solve it together.* Let go of the need to be right. Be on the lookout for win-win solutions—but be ready to compromise, if necessary.

3. *Respect each person's right to his or her own opinions and feelings.* There's no point in arguing with another person's perceptions. For each of us, our perceptions are real *for the frame of mind we are in.* Instead of trying to change someone's perspective, stay cool and remain patient as thoughts are shared and emotions are expressed.

4. *Generate lots of creative ideas that might solve the problem without critiquing them as you go.* What could all parties do to resolve the issue? Where is your common ground? What does everyone want from this situation? Do not edit or judge the ideas produced during brainstorming. Creativity often generates some unworkable ideas before the good ones come. Just write down any possible solutions that come to mind without criticizing them as "stupid," "unrealistic," or "crazy." Record both parties' thoughts until you have a list of options.

5. *Evaluate the various options.* Cut the ones you don't want to try. Discuss the pros and cons of the best ones.

6. *Make a choice.* Which solutions do all parties like best?

7. *Define the solution as specifically as possible.* What does the solu-

tion require from every party? Is the solution reasonable and realistic? Is it what you want?

8. *Check back later to see if the solution is working.* If not, try another idea.

So, how did Sophia and Larry resolve their issues?

Through their Taking Turns Conversation, Sophia and Larry had accomplished points 1, 2, and 3. Here's the list of possible solutions they generated and how they evaluated each of them.

Idea	Comment	Evaluation
Wait to make changes until after Paul graduates.	Sophia picks up the burden of their decision.	Not good
Tell Paul he needs to restrict his college choices to what they can afford.	One of the reasons they limited their family to one child was so they could give that child the best educational start. Paul is bright and will benefit.	Not good
Sell the furniture store and let Larry find a job.	The furniture store has been in the family for years; it does good business most years.	Potentially helpful but disruptive

Buy a Powerball ticket.	Imaginative but unlikely to pay off.	Not good
Take a second mortgage on the house to pay for college.	Mortgages are difficult to get, and there's a long-term financial risk.	Potentially helpful but high risk.
Put Sophia to work at the store, doing marketing.	Her advice would be helpful, but there's not enough money to pay her what she earns freelancing.	Not good
Rent space in the house.	There will be an extra room available when Paul goes to college, and if Sophia gets a job, her home office will also be available.	Potentially helpful but would change their lifestyle

They decided to let Sophia apply for a full-time job with one of her clients and to discuss the offer, if she got one. As it turned out, she found a position that paid a bit more than her freelance income and had opportunity for growth. When she could, she helped out with marketing ideas for Larry's furniture store. They decided to reconsider the rental issue, once they had more information about the cost of Paul's college and the state of their budget as the time got closer. In the meantime, they closed up Sophia's home office—with access from the garage—making it available to a potential tenant.

Five Brainstorming DOs

When participating in a Win-Win Solution Brainstorming session, keep the following guidelines in mind:

1. Work as a team.
2. Be open to everyone's input.
3. Address one issue at a time.
4. Focus on having everyone win.
5. Have a set time limit (20–30 minutes).

Solving Circles

Another useful conflict-resolution strategy is called "Solving Circles," developed using renowned psychiatrist Dr. William Glasser's choice theory. Let's see how it works. The Solving Circles technique is most easily understood as a graphic. On a piece of paper, sketch two overlapping circles. (This is a traditional Venn diagram.) Label the first circle "Party A." Label the second circle "Party B." Your drawing should look like the following image:

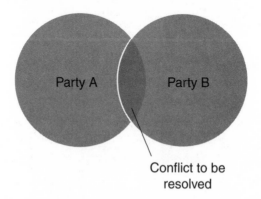

Conflict to be
resolved

The area where the two circles intersect represents the conflict to be resolved between the two parties.

During a conflict, people tend to tell each other how to behave; the suggestion is that the other person must change. Solving Circles takes a different approach. The two parties negotiate from inside their own circles or realms of responsibility. Party A identifies and communicates the steps he or she will take to solve the problem. Party B responds in kind, describing what he or she will do to remedy the situation. Even challenging conflicts can be resolved in this manner because each party (1) reflects on the issue and (2) takes responsibility for his or her actions. Participants realize they can change only themselves, and not the other person.

When you use the Solving Circles strategy, do not rehash history. Bringing up memories keeps you rooted in the past—which you can't change with any measures you take now. Instead, keep the discussion focused on the future, where the problem can be fixed.

To conclude, the Solving Circles approach works because the participants do not find fault with each other or tell each other what to do. They maintain their self-respect while exercising self-responsibility. In this manner, problems are solved quickly, improving personal relationships.

Forms of Conflict Resolution

The solution to a problem may take several forms. While re-solving a conflict through *consensus* is typically the ideal, *compromise* and *negotiation* have their uses, as well.

- *Consensus.* In a consensus, the parties in a conflict arrive at a mutual agreement and a common understanding. Consensus requires reflection, creativity, and tolerance. Typically, a solution achieved through consensus is strong. All participants believe in the solution, which preserves their dignity and reinforces their relationship.
- *Compromise.* In a compromise, a dispute is resolved through concessions made by both parties. That is, each party gives up something it desires until both parties are equally satisfied with the result. Compromise necessitates open-mind-

edness and consideration. Like consensus, compromise typically preserves participants' dignity.

- *Negotiation.* In a negotiation, the conflicting parties hear each other out to understand both points of view. They evaluate options for fixing the problem, pointing out advantages and disadvantages. Ultimately, the parties come to an agreement on the terms of a solution. Each side seeks to gain a personal benefit by the end of the dialogue.

Guidelines for Addressing a Felt Injustice

In some conflicts, one party may feel that the other's behavior has resulted in an injustice. The relationship of Meg and Tim in Key 3 is an excellent example. Meg was taking on responsibility for Tim's children as well as her own, handling all the work involved in maintaining the household, and working part time. She never complained—that was part of her passive-aggressive approach to life—but she nevertheless felt that she was being unfairly burdened. Her attempts to communicate her distress in a passive-aggressive style—first, by making herself sick, and later, by ignoring his children—were having no impact on the overall situation.

It seems clear that the marriage between Meg and Tim will falter under the strain of her anger and his refusal to attend to her needs. Although her passive-aggressive style may make it difficult, she can approach this issue directly and seek redress. Here's how it would work.

1. *Give yourself time between the triggering incident and your talk so that you can calm down or gain clarity and also alert your partner to the problem.* When Meg became sick because of the extra strain of caring for his children over the weekend, she might say to Tim, "I'm sick because of the extra effort and stress involved in caring for your children. I need time to think it through. Let's chat about it tomorrow morning, okay?"

2. *At the intended time of your talk, assess whether the other person is in the proper mindset to give the matter serious attention.* Say, "I need to talk to you about how we're going to care properly for your children with Georgia. Do you feel this is a good time to hear what I have to say?" If your partner says no, ask for an alternative time.

3. *Approach the issue with the intent of preserving the relationship.* Think about how you can describe the problem in a way that will benefit your relationship. For instance, Meg can say, "Part of our marriage is the children we each brought to it separately. I want us to enjoy each other's children and feel like we are all part of a family. In order to get there, I need to explain how caring for them is affecting me and how much I would value your help."

4. *Don't punish the other person.* Avoid name-calling and insults. Don't scold. It won't help if Meg says: "You're always running off when your kids are here, though I can't blame you—they're little brats." In addition, be aware that, because of your anger, your personal energy might come across as punishing. If you stay present in the moment and keep in mind your love for the other person, you can avoid this pitfall.

5. *Stick to the subject.* Explain how you have been feeling about the incident. Remember to use "I" statements. For example, "I have taken on too much responsibility. Between my household chores and my extra job and my own three kids, I'm already pressed to my limit. When your kids show up on the weekend, I just don't have the energy to handle them on my own. I need some help."

6. *Include positive details.* Mention things the other person did right, too. For instance, Meg might say, "I know how hard you are working, with two jobs, to provide for our family." Or you might offer alternative views of what happened. "I've never spoken of this before, so I'm not surprised that you haven't noticed my problems. You have a lot on your mind."

7. *Note how the other person is responding to your comments.* His or her body language will provide you with feedback. If the person is becoming angry or defensive, adjust your approach.

8. *Tell the other person the change you'd like to see.* Paint a positive picture of what you *do* want and let him or her know why it is important to you. For example, Meg might say, "I would appreciate it if you could be around when your children are with us. It would be good for the kids to have all seven of us together. I know you're trying to be a good father, and they need some of your attention." Ask the other person to paraphrase what you've said so you can make sure your request is understood. Meanwhile, keep in mind that the other person will need to *decide* to change. You can, however, protect yourself from such behavior by setting limits based on your own boundaries and seeing if the person is willing to respect them.

9. *Provide feedback later.* As soon as you see improvement, acknowledge it. Use specific recognition of the change you see instead of general praise. For instance, Meg might eventually say, "Thank you for being home Saturday. I know the children— mine and yours—were happy for the outing to the beach, and I really loved having all seven of us around the table for dinner." If you see no change, ask the other person to give further consideration to your request.

10. *Continue to monitor this type of interaction.* Thank the other person for fulfilling your request. If your original solution doesn't work, think of alternate approaches you can use.

For Meg and Tim, the problem has grown to crisis proportions, and they may need the help of a marriage counselor or other professional to help them work through their issues. Not all injustices are this complicated, however, and discussing the problem is better than letting the anger fester.

The Art of Apology

Why do we feel the need for an apology when someone's actions cause us emotional pain or disappointment? When an offense occurs, we want to know the offender understands that we were upset as a result. If an apology *is* forthcoming, we want to feel that it's sincere—that the other person is truly sorry for hurting our feelings. Excuses and counterfeit admissions of guilt can make matters worse by leaving us feeling invalidated.

Those who learn they have done an injustice to another need to apologize. While this begins with words, it has to involve more than lip service. What the offended person really wants is different behavior. The words are the promise of change, but the supporting actions are the proof.

This can be especially difficult for people who engage in passive-aggressive behavior. They are willing, even eager, to apologize, but the proof that is supposed to follow the promise may not be forthcoming. Part of being in a relationship means caring about the effects your choices and actions have on others. Do your best to learn from your mistakes and make sure you don't repeat them. By doing so, your relationships and your self-esteem will blossom.

There are right and wrong ways to apologize. So how can you do it correctly when someone has a grievance against you? The steps below will walk you through a helpful approach.

1. *Be truly sorry that you upset the other party.* Even if you wouldn't be hurt by the same behavior, understand that this person was. In the case of Meg and Tim, he may not be aware he has upset her—she never complains.

2. *Acknowledge the hurt done and take responsibility for making amends.* Describe specifically what happened, and make it clear you understand what was upsetting about it. Validate the other person's feelings by repeating what's been said and commenting on what you notice. For example, Tim might say, "I can see that I've left you with too much responsibility for our family, especially my children. I'm sorry for the physical pain this is causing, and I'm even sorrier that you've felt alone with all of this work." Add something like, "I am truly sorry. I shouldn't have done that. How can I make this right?"

3. *Commit to not letting it happen again.* Let the person know that

you've learned from this mistake and that you'll change your behavior. Provide specifics about what you realize and what you'll do differently. Tim needs to consider how he can ease the childcare burdens on Meg while ensuring that the family has the financial resources it needs. This may involve staying home when his children join the family on weekends or providing extra household help for Meg. Using the techniques discussed in this chapter, the two of them will need to discuss how they can improve the situation.

If you are involved in a passive-aggressive loop, you may need to take steps to ensure that the injustice is not repeated. This may involve checking in with yourself *every day* to ensure that you have kept your commitments, or asking your partner to raise a flag immediately if he or she senses a new transgression about to happen.

4. *Express appreciation for having the other person in your life.* Tell your family member how important the relationship is to you. This is especially important for Tim and Meg. He might say, "I am so proud to have you for my wife, and you have been a wonderful mother to your kids and mine. I don't know what I would do without you."

5. *Ask for forgiveness.* By making a request for forgiveness, you are reinforcing your earlier message that the relationship is important to you. You are also allowing the offended party to decide the outcome of the exchange—which can be challenging for you. Realize that the offended person may need some time to decide, especially in the case of a major transgression.

6. *Follow through with the improved behavior.* To regain the other person's trust, be true to your word and clean up your act. Ask yourself, "What is my plan to ensure that this transgression does not happen again?" Good intentions are often not enough to change habitual behavior. You have to be mindful and committed. Putting something in writing, either in your journal or perhaps in a datebook—just a note to remind you of your commitment—can help you catch yourself and "stay awake" so you don't slip back unconsciously into the behavior.

Separating the Past from the Present

A discussion of conflict resolution would be incomplete without reiterating that the present is influenced by the past. Very often, what we think is an upset in a current situation is really unfinished business from the past. Eighty percent of our emotional upset surrounds our childhood wounds—the original charge. When you are working toward resolving conflicts with partners, employers, friends, or coworkers, take a look at yourself. Determine if the issue at hand is something you've experienced before. The following exercise may help you identify the role of past hurts in present conflicts.

Exercise: Are Your Conflicts About the Past?

1. Recall a recent situation in which you were in conflict with someone.
2. Review similar incidents. See if you can recognize a pattern. Ask yourself the following questions: How do you behave at these times? What are you feeling? How does the other person act? How does he or she seem to be feeling?
3. Identify experiences in your past that match this pattern or otherwise seem to relate to the present issue. When have you felt this way before? Think about the meaning you have given to the earlier events. How do you think they affect you today? What thoughts and feelings do you experience as you remember them?
4. With your new awareness, mindfully watch for upcoming situations involving the same issue. When you notice yourself being triggered, pause and reflect on your emotional response. Identify the feelings and experience them. At the same time, stay centered and attempt to make better choices about how you interact with the other person.

People with old emotional wounds—and those who suffer from passive-aggressiveness almost always have them—don't have to be stuck with old responses. By becoming self-reflective and mindful, you can begin to view your past in a new way. And by using the strategies outlined in this key, you can start to create better resolutions. You will also experience a greater feeling of aliveness as you become more open to the truth of the present.

Advice for Partners

Using the conflict resolution techniques in this chapter can make a remarkable change in your relationship with those who have passive-aggressive behavior patterns. First of all, the structures provide a support that can lift you out of the confusing muddle that partners often feel when they are on the receiving end of passive-aggressive behavior. For example, part of the passive-aggressive syndrome is to project anger onto others, such that the person who is passive-aggressive will feel that you are angry with him or her when the reverse is true. The person may also provoke you to express your anger and then use that explosion to justify his or her feelings of victimhood. This leaves you feeling not only angry but also guilty about it at the same time.

In Key 6, you have a variety of objective and effective ways to uncover the hidden conflicts in your relationship that may be causing some of the strange responses you're getting from your partner. These strategies are designed to be as nonthreatening as possible to the person locked in a passive-aggressive cycle. The idea is to assure your partner that they can express their true feelings and discuss them with you in a calm and reasonable way.

Instead of seeing their anger and your disagreements as dangers to the relationship, they can be persuaded, with time, that anger and conflict, when properly expressed and handled, can open the door to the intimacy and security they are seeking.

You will need to take the lead here, both by initiating these conflict resolution strategies when unspoken conflicts seem to be simmering beneath the surface of your relationship and by insisting that disagreements be discussed within the frameworks and rules described here.

INTERACT USING MINDFULNESS

To their friends Thomas and Cindy, Alan and Barbara seemed like a typical couple in a long-term marriage—25 years and still counting—until Alan started complaining to Thomas about Barbara's reckless spending, her weight gain, her lack of interest in travel.

Thomas shared the complaints with his wife, Cindy. "Why doesn't he say these things to his wife?" Cindy asked. "You can't do anything about it, but she could."

Thomas shook his head. "He says she won't listen. Every time he mentions anything the least bit critical, she gets upset and accuses him of wanting to leave her for another woman."

"Alan is a nice guy, a straight arrow," Cindy said. "I can't see him having an affair."

But, eventually, Alan did. The marriage was over, and their mutual friends tended to blame Alan and stick with Barbara. The truth was much more complicated. From the earliest days of their marriage, Barbara had expressed her anger and fears about the relationship by buying things they couldn't afford and running up credit card bills. When she refused to discuss their budget issues, Alan would rebuke her sarcastically: "Could you please use your gold card to buy some cat food," he might say, "since that's all we'll be able to afford after I pay your bill?"

Barbara didn't see her behavior as passive-aggressive, and Alan didn't understand that he was playing into her hand, giving her new cause for hurt feelings. Still, they were caught

*in a devastating cycle. As they got older and Barbara felt even
less secure, she found herself gaining weight. She turned down
his suggestions of travel, sure that he was just looking for an
excuse to meet women.*

*In the end, Alan had an affair with a woman from his of-
fice. It wasn't the sex that drew him—although that quickly
became a pleasurable part of the relationship—so much as
having someone he could talk to about his life and his feelings. Seeing how he related to this new woman, he understood
what his marriage had been missing all these years: honest
and open communication.*

*Even then, however, instead of telling Barbara how he felt,
he waited until she stumbled on the new couple at a restaurant. She flew into a fury of pent-up rage, accusing him of
trying to drive her crazy so he could put her in an institution.
Alan moved out, and the divorce quickly followed. They never
talked about what had been slowly eroding the foundations of
their marriage for many years.*

Because they couldn't get past reactive, hurtful responses to
their emotions, Alan and Barbara lost a long-term marriage. The
problem began with Barbara and her reactive behavior, which
followed a passive-aggressive pattern she had developed in childhood. Afraid to express her anger and equally fearful of the conflict that could flow from any disagreement, Barbara had allowed
her negative feelings to leak out in ways that were emotionally
abusive, not only to Alan but to their children as well. Yet she
didn't see that she had any responsibility for the breakup of her
marriage. In fact, she thought she had done everything she could
to "keep the peace," only to experience the betrayal she had always expected.

Alan played his part in the breakup as well, by falling into step
with the passive-aggressive pattern his wife established. When she
reacted with alarm to his efforts at fruitful discussion, he backed
away from conflict, when in fact conflict was the only way the two
of them could take the steps necessary to save their marriage.

In Key 7, we will look at the challenges of passive-aggressiveness
from the point of view of the person who brings that issue into the

relationship. Then, in Key 8, we will take up those challenges from the perspective of her or his partners—lovers, spouses, friends, children, parents, employers, and coworkers.

The Dangers of Reactive Behavior

Passive-aggressive behavior wreaks havoc on the emotional lives of everyone it touches. It may be most harmful, however, to the people who—consciously or unconsciously—are setting this pattern for their relationships. Rewarding connections are incompatible with the suppressed emotions and restricted communication that are part of the passive-aggressive personality pattern. Although their marriage was difficult for both Alan and Barbara, Alan moved on to a more promising relationship while Barbara retreated, more than ever convinced of her victimhood even though she herself had set the sad outcome in motion.

The fact is that passive-aggression is a reactive approach to life, a topic we've touched on in Keys 3 and 4. When someone says or does something that makes us feel threatened, this triggers our fight-or-flight mechanism, flooding our bodies with stress hormones. One consequence of this is that the reasoning part of the brain, the neocortex, shuts down. Instead of responding rationally or thoughtfully to what's happening, we attack or deny, avoid or run away.

When your reactive mode is triggered, you can feel it in your body:

- Your heart pounds, and your pulse races.
- You continue to speak while the other person is talking.
- Your goal is not to communicate but to win.
- You turn trivial things into causes for battle.

When you're reactive, you're not paying attention to the other person—or even to yourself. You're not conscious of your words, tone of voice, or body language, and you don't see how they are affecting the other person. You're on "automatic pilot," and while you might feel yourself getting enraged, you're powerless to stop it. You want to shut the other person down and make her or him the problem. It's easy to see how a relationship in which both partners are habitually reactive can become a war zone and be doomed to failure.

Passive-aggressive behavior destroys relationships in a variety of ways. Individuals who adopt passive-aggressive behavior are unlikely to see their contribution to what happens to their relationships, so let's look more closely at outcomes.

The End of Communication and Intimacy

Alan and Barbara are an excellent example of this outcome. Characterized by denial, evasiveness, and blaming, passive-aggression seems designed to make those who encounter such behavior explode with thoughtless anger. Being asked about their feelings or motives can make people suffering from passive-aggressiveness feel as if they're under assault, so they're always on guard. Their partners, frustrated that their latest attempt to calmly discuss the problem has been met with a roll of the eyes, lose their cool and snap, reacting with sarcasm or rage. When one partner in a relationship is passive-aggressive, bringing up the problems that behavior creates may turn a calm discussion into a shouting match. After a while, both partners may begin to feel that the other person will never listen and doesn't care about solving her or his problems.

When that happens, communication stops. Of course, for those who are passive-aggressive, this only reinforces the idea that they need to be defensive, and around and around we go.

An Environment of Fear

When one or both partners have reactive communication styles, they can become time bombs of rage primed to go off at the slightest provocation. Whether each partner actually does this doesn't matter. What matters is that one or both believe that they have to walk on eggshells around each other or risk being verbally assaulted. In this kind of abusive environment, both partners live in apprehension that the next thing they say or do will be the thing that provokes a screaming match.

> *Angela is the publisher of a successful consumer health magazine. She thinks of herself as a demanding boss, but her editorial and design staff see her as a hypercritical, passive-aggressive abuser. Angela gives vague instructions to her writers and designers and never clearly states what she's looking for. Then, if the resulting work doesn't meet her standards (which seem to change weekly), she rips the work apart and makes the person do it again. And again. By making everyone worry about working extra hours, she controls the office through fear.*
>
> *If a writer or designer takes issue with having to redo perfectly good work, or if he or she asks for more specific directions, Angela explodes. No matter how diplomatic the person is, she fears that her authority is being challenged. She threatens, rants, and raves. New employees quickly learn that the office environment is toxic. Many of them—especially the brightest—leave as quickly as possible. The rest keep their heads down and try to do work that's least likely to provoke Angela. Nobody takes creative risks because no one wants to turn a 40-hour workweek into 80 frustrating hours trying to please her. As a result, the magazine is stale and turnover is sky high.*

At least employees have the option of finding another job. Imagine how this approach would devastate children.

A Roadblock to Progress

Without communication, conflict will never be resolved and the situation will never improve. When someone is conditioned to react, honest criticism becomes character assassination. With a hypersensitive, passive-aggressive person, even a neutral statement like "Your sister got a promotion at work, and she's really thrilled" can provoke a reaction like "And I suppose that makes me the black sheep. I never was the smart one." Such relationships become riddled with wounds that are never allowed to heal.

> *Frank is a retired logger, a rough, tough man's man, and he's never really accepted the fact that his only son, Kyle, is gay. Frank doesn't say anything openly, but he takes passive-aggressive steps to "get back" at Kyle for not being his idea of a macho man. Frank cancels get-togethers, makes snide remarks to Kyle's boyfriends, and "forgets" to sign birthday cards his wife buys. After years of these slight offenses, Kyle won't speak to his father.*
>
> *Hannah, Kyle's older sister, has spent a year trying to broker peace between the two. More than once, she's persuaded Kyle to agree to meet on neutral ground—a restaurant—for a "clear the air" discussion with Frank. But Frank never shows up. In his mind, he's done nothing wrong, and at the same time, he feels ashamed. Several times, Hannah has started careful, compassionate talks with him, only to see them turn into shouting matches that send her running to her car in tears. Because Frank can't (or won't) consciously address his homophobia and his embarrassment over how he's treated Kyle, he risks losing his son forever, and perhaps his daughter as well.*

As we saw in Key 6, conflict is a way to heal wounds and increase connection and intimacy. When fear of conflict takes over, hope for the relationship becomes dimmer and dimmer.

No Responsibility, No Power

When you communicate reactively, you give the other person's words power to determine your emotional responses and your behavior. Rather than examining what people say to make sure you understand their meaning, you leap to an emotional conclusion. Instead of letting the conversation reveal the person's intent, you respond as if you need to defend yourself. This powerless posture is often part of the passive-aggressive pattern, and it leads to the result that you are confirmed in your feelings of victimhood. The world *is* out to get you, and the best you can do is duck.

A more insidious outcome is that as you surrender power, you also persuade yourself that you have no responsibility for what is said and what is done as a result of your encounter. You hold yourself innocent and place all the blame on others. Barbara's husband betrayed her. Angela's employees are incompetent and disrespectful. Frank's son is embarrassing his father with his gay lifestyle.

The truth is far different. People who engage in passive-aggressive behavior have enormous power over themselves and others, and they can begin to improve their lives and their relationships *only* when they accept responsibility for what they say and do.

Take Responsibility

Let's be clear: I am asking you to take responsibility for your harmful and destructive *actions*. I am not saying that *you* are harmful and destructive. In fact, you may suffer from these actions as much as or more than the people with whom you interact. Nevertheless, until you take responsibility for what you're doing, nothing can change. No understanding partner, no new job, no professional counselor—no one and nothing can help to resolve your passive-aggressive behavior until you sign on.

You deserve to be happy. You deserve the joy and support that comes from honest and sound relationships. To achieve these outcomes, you need to understand that you are the biggest roadblock standing in your way. Change is always a challenge, and changing ingrained behavior that has served you since childhood is going to be hard work. Still, it's the most meaningful and rewarding work a person can do. It can help you pull existing relationships out of the ditch you've run them into or create healthier relationships now and in the future.

First, you will need to *accept responsibility* for what *you* do that needs to change. You need to look at yourself honestly and examine your behavior rigorously. Once you've identified the problem areas, you need to make a firm and enduring commitment to achieving change. You can change only yourself—but that is enough. That's all you have to do for things to improve—but it is the only thing that can provide that good outcome.

I say again: First, you will need to *accept responsibility* for what happens to you and how you feel about it. That's extremely hard to do for people stuck in the passive-aggressive loop. You have an excuse or an explanation for everything. You see attack where none was intended, and you're ready to defend yourself even before a criticism has been made. You see yourself from a narrow, self-serving perspective that prevents you from looking at your words and actions honestly and dispassionately.

If you are late for an appointment, consider whether you should have started earlier, not whether the bus was on time or the traffic was heavy. If you get a poor grade on an assignment, don't blame it on the teacher: Did you follow instructions, did you give the project enough time, did you review your work carefully? If someone seems angry with you, consider the possibility that she or he has a good reason. Ask—sincerely—what you did wrong. Or examine your behavior to see what might have been displeasing.

Take responsibility for your own feelings as well. In Keys 2 and 3, you learned how to identify your feelings accurately. Say you were hoping to go to a movie, but your friend would prefer to see a concert. This is not a case where *your friend* is disappointing you or commenting on your taste. It simply means that you have different goals for a particular evening. It's a normal everyday kind of dispute that can be resolved using the strategies in Key 6. If you feel bad about it, you're the problem, not your friend.

Remember that as you accept responsibility, you will also be taking back the power over your life that you have given away. You can become the kind of person you want to be, knowing who you are and having the strength to ask for what you need. That change must begin inside. Much of this book has been about reconnecting with your feelings and discarding the old thought patterns that are harmful and untrue. In Key 3 we talked about mindfulness. This strategy for living in the present is the most crucial tool in the transformation you must make.

That's because you can't change what you aren't aware of, and you can become aware of something only by *being* aware and in the present, noticing what you're doing and what's going on both within you and around you. As we said in Key 3, being mindful is your responsibility: How much or little awareness you bring to your life is entirely up to you. Mindfulness is both a practice and a skill; it is the opposite of reactive behavior.

Using Mindfulness to Change

Being mindful anchors us in the present. It makes us acutely aware of what we're saying, how we're feeling, and how our words and actions are affecting others. This self-awareness lets us slow down our responses and gain conscious control of what has been pure reflex.

Mindfulness helps people become more aware of their passive-aggressive behavior and the defense mechanisms they use to dodge responsibility. The exercises in Key 3 can help you learn simple techniques for getting responses under control and become aware of the healthier and more constructive responses you can make.

With passive-aggressive behavior, you look at what *the other person is doing to you*. But with mindfulness, you go into yourself to understand what *you are doing to you*. You drop down beyond your thoughts to understand the meaning of what you're feeling. I advise my patients to sit quietly, breathing, focused but without judgment, following their breath and seeing what their feelings tell them.

By teaching yourself to be mindful of your emotions and your biological responses to them, you give yourself the power to pause. You create space between your triggers and your response. You slow down your response to reflect. You gain the time to notice the knot forming in your stomach and ask, "What is that trying to tell me?" You respond consciously and constructively to the other person instead of engaging in the defensive and evasive responses typical of passive-aggression.

Mindfulness can transform a relationship torn apart by passive-aggression:

- It helps both partners overcome negative emotional habits like avoidance, blaming, and defensiveness that do nothing but perpetuate the passive-aggressive cycle.
- It lets you feel and release your anger by expressing it rationally and nonjudgmentally.
- It helps you consciously choose language and actions that deescalate potential conflicts, defuse anger, and reassert your goals—resolution, not destruction, as described in Key 6.
- It puts powerful tools like assertiveness, gentle humor, self-deprecation, compassion, empathy, and respect back on the table.
- It helps you to really listen and respond to what the other person is saying, not your interpretation of what she or he is saying.
- If you are in a relationship with a passive-aggressive person, it helps you to communicate with her or him at the first signs of passive-aggression, helping you defuse the situation before it gets out of control.

We give small children time-outs when they're upset. It gives them a chance to calm down and regain control. Mindfulness is just an adult time-out. It gives us a chance to see what that knot in our stomach or lump in our throat is all about, so we can do something positive.

Exercise: How Mindful Are You?

Choose the number from 1 to 5 that indicates how strongly you agree or disagree with the statement about your tendency to communicate reactively.

1. In a conversation or disagreement, I focus my attention on what I am doing rather than on what my partner is doing.

Strongly   1   2   3   4   5   Strongly
disagree   agree

2. In a disagreement, I listen actively instead of thinking only about what I will say when the other person is finally done speaking.

Strongly   1   2   3   4   5   Strongly
disagree   agree

3. I am good at slowing my thinking down so that I can observe my own thoughts, feelings, words, and actions objectively.

Strongly   1   2   3   4   5   Strongly
disagree   agree

4. In a confrontation, I am able to regard my own thoughts and words and those of my partner with acceptance and calm.

Strongly   1   2   3   4   5   Strongly
disagree   agree

5. I am also able to look at my and my partner's words and actions as they really are without relating them to my ego—not making it "about me."

Strongly   1   2   3   4   5   Strongly
disagree   agree

6. No matter what I observe during a disagreement or confrontation, I keep it in the present. I don't attach baggage from the past or future.

Strongly   1   2   3   4   5   Strongly
disagree   agree

7. I'm consistently able to notice how my thoughts, feelings, and sensations change during a conversation or disagreement.

Strongly   1   2   3   4   5   Strongly
disagree   agree

8. I'm consistently able to consciously choose how I will respond to my experiences during a conversation or disagreement.

| Strongly disagree | 1 | 2 | 3 | 4 | 5 | Strongly agree |

Now, take a moment to journal any other thoughts you have about your own mindful or reactive tendencies.

Add up your score. If you scored from 32 to 40, you are probably acting with great mindfulness in your relationships. On the other hand, if you scored from 8 to 16, you may be sabotaging your relationships with reactive behaviors. If you scored between 17 and 32, then you are probably like many people, a mix of mindfulness on some occasions and reactivity on others.

Identifying the Problem

Half of the solution is identifying the problem. You can't change what you don't acknowledge as your responsibility. Here are some typical issues related to passive-aggressive behavior. With a mindful attitude and an openness to accepting responsibility, take a look and see which of these behaviors may be contributing to problems in your relationships. They fall into three clusters: unresponsive responses, active inaction, and communicative isolation.

Unresponsive Responses

A key feature of passive-aggressive behavior is *defensiveness* in the face of challenges, even those that are imagined. Some of this involves *direct denial*. For example, say your neighbor has asked you to look in on her cats while she's away, and she reads from your body language that you're not eager to help.

NEIGHBOR: You seem concerned. Is this too much? Are you busy with other things? Are you okay with cats?

You: Cats are okay. I'm sure I can find a few minutes to take care of them.

Neighbor: I don't want to put you out.

You: Of course, you don't. It's fine.

Another element is having a ready *excuse or rationalization* for your behavior. Suppose your neighbor comes home and finds dry food spilled all over the floor. The next time she sees you, she asks you what happened. You might say, "They seemed really upset about my coming in, so I just put out the dry food and didn't bother them again." Or, "You know, I sneezed something terrible the first time I visited. I think I left them enough food to get along." Either way, you come out looking good: Whether you're sensitive to cat behavior or simply allergic to cats, how can your neighbor complain?

Sulking and self-pity are other characteristics of the passive-aggressive personality pattern. Sulkers let everyone know just how unhappy they are, but they'll deny it if asked. Self-pity is more internal. Taken to its logical conclusion, it leads to *victimhood thinking*, where people feel that everyone is taking advantage of them or that they are being slighted by life itself. If it's true, that's because they haven't spoken up about their needs and boundaries.

Active Inaction

Another set of passive-aggressive behaviors involves action performed in a way that tends to work against the original goals. Given directions by a teacher or other authority figure, a child might engage in *hostile or temporary compliance*, performing the task but with a negative attitude or working on the task only until the teacher turns away. *Lack of follow-through* is a variation on this: I agree to do something, but I don't complete the task. Or, in *procrastination*, I put it off until it's too late to get done on time or done well— or someone else does it. *Intentional inefficiency* means doing the assignment but so badly that no one will ever ask again. Sometimes the passive-aggressive *fear of competition* expresses itself this way, by portraying oneself as barely competent, although Angela, with her excessive demands, also displays this response.

Obstructionism takes it one step further. Instead of foot-dragging, this behavior actually works against completion of the task. Your friend wants to go to a play you're not eager to see, so you're not ready when it's time to leave, and you forget something crucial so you have to return home. *Chronic lateness and forgetfulness* are part of this pattern. Passive-aggressive behavior may also include *conscious or unconscious retaliation or revenge.*

Communicative Isolation

Some of the communication issues in this cluster are familiar: *lack of empathy* or *failure to be present*, sometimes expressed as *not listening*. These work against making honest and open connections in a relationship. They reveal the passive-aggressive fear of intimacy, a reluctance to show oneself for fear of rejection. That also plays a role in passive-aggressive styles of conversation, like *ambiguity* about plans or ideas, staying on the fence for fear of doing the wrong thing, simply muttering or talking in a way that's confusing or hard to understand, or changing the subject or point the other is trying to make. In conflict, the passive-aggressive role is often to avoid the topic altogether.

A larger problem of passive-aggressive behavior is *negativity.* "Yes, but," is a marker phrase of passive-aggression. These are the people who see the hole instead of the doughnut, and boy, that hole is a monster. People who suffer with passive-aggression are suspicious of others, and they view the world as a hostile place. This negativity touches virtually every part of their lives. You may want to tell me that you have a lot of reasons to be unhappy. Let me remind you that Abraham Lincoln is said to have remarked, "Most people are as happy as they make up their mind to be." Certainly, everyone has difficult times, but happiness is as much a state of mind as a factual situation.

Understanding Why

If you have identified passive-aggressive behaviors in your life—and if you approached the last section honestly with an openness to accepting responsibility, you saw yourself here—then you may be feeling puzzled. Having finally seen your behavior the way other people see you, it's not surprising if you are confronted with the same question they have: *Why* do you do these things?

Now it's time to return to the various exercises you learned in Keys 1, 2, and 3 and to get in touch with your anger and the feelings it reveals, to examine your habitual thoughts, and to use the techniques of mindfulness on your inner emotional life.

Chances are you are suffering the consequences of fears that are typical in passive-aggression:

- Fear of competition
- Fear of dependency
- Fear of abandonment
- Fear of intimacy
- Fear of vulnerability

Note how these fears play against each other. At the same time that you're afraid your partner will leave you, you're also afraid to show the vulnerability that can draw the two of you together into a more intimate relationship. You're afraid of becoming dependent on someone else, but you also shy away from competition. You always seem to find yourself between a rock and a hard place.

Exercise: Writing for Discovery

Here is a way to see yourself from a different perspective.

1. Pretend you are writing a novel. Create a character who will represent you and another character who will represent your

partner. Describe them. They don't have to look like "the real people," but they should have the same basic characteristics.

2. Now write a scene that describes the last time you and your partner had a difficult encounter.

3. Describe the triggering event in detail. Remember that your reader wasn't there, so include everything about the scene.

4. Novels tell you what the characters are feeling and thinking, not just what they say and do. Add these elements to your story.

5. If you're not clear on what you were feeling, revisit Key 3. By sitting quietly and recalling the encounter, you can examine the sensations in your body and see what thoughts, feelings, memories, or images were associated with them.

6. This is a novel, so you can use your imagination. To represent what your partner was thinking and feeling, you will need to exercise empathy. Put yourself inside your partner's character and imagine his or her thoughts and reactions.

7. A big part of fiction is motivation. Looking at the characters and the situation you've set up, what should happen next? Why?

8. Asking the same questions again and again, go through the encounter step by step. Let your story develop to its conclusion.

9. Because this is fiction, the encounter can end differently than the real outcome did. If it does, look at what you've written to see what changed.

10. You can also critique the written encounter. Did your character display any of the characteristic behaviors of passive-aggressiveness? Why? What other responses were possible? Rewrite the scene again to see how it comes out with the passive-aggressive responses changed.

Understanding why you have adopted passive-aggressive behavior doesn't provide an explanation or excuse for continuing on that road. On the contrary, it opens the door to the possibility of change.

Making a Commitment to Change

Now that you have accepted responsibility for what happens in your life, identified your passive-aggressive behaviors, and explored why this has been your chosen response, the moment for change has arrived. Please note that accepting responsibility was the *first* step, although it fits here, too. Without an attitude that is open to personal responsibility, however, the other parts of the process would not be fruitful. You could still be pointing fingers away from the person who has sole responsibility for your life and its outcome: you.

Now it is time to *enact* that attitude of responsibility, taking charge of making the changes that will transform your life, revive old relationships, and open the door to intimacy with old partners or new. Mindfulness is your best friend in meeting this challenge. Pay attention to what you're doing, feeling, and saying moment by moment. Vigilance is especially important when you find yourself in a conflict or the other person is becoming upset with you. Always take that as a wakeup call, letting you know you've fallen back asleep.

Prepare a Plan

While making an emotional and intellectual commitment to change is essential, this challenge is too large to rely only on an abstract willingness to move forward with your life in a different way. You need a plan.

Earlier, I asked you to identify the passive-aggressive behaviors that have been a part of your life. Now I'd like you to make a list of these behaviors and select the handful that seem to be most common or to cause you and those you enact them on the most trouble. Using a paper notebook or a digital format, create a journal. For each behavior, describe the circumstances that seem to trigger it and the other person who is most affected. It might look something like this.

Behavior	Triggers	Motivations	Person(s) Affected
Being late	Group meetings at the office	Meetings make me anxious. My fear of competition tells me I'm going to look bad in comparison to the others.	Employer, coworkers
Lack of follow-through	Group projects—I never get my part done on time.	I'm uncertain about what to do and afraid my work won't be good enough. It's easier if I can see what everyone else has done first.	Employer, coworkers

Now make a second chart that assesses your behavioral motivations and provides a goal to conquer the objectionable passive-aggressive behavior. When you set a goal, go for it! Push for the best you can be. When we need to lose weight, we often start with a particularly rigorous diet. That helps us get used to the new behavior of "eating less." Along the way, we might be able to ease back just a bit, but we need the strict rules of a diet to put us on the right path. Here's how your second chart might look.

Behavior	Assessment of Motivation	New Goals
Being late	I'm afraid of meeting because I think the others will make me look bad, but being late *always* makes me look bad.	Be the first person in the door for meetings. Take the extra time while others are assembling to calm yourself with some deep, cleansing breaths and to organize your thoughts about the topic to be discussed.
Lack of follow-through	I'm always late with my piece of the project because I want to see what others have done first. Falling in behind the others makes me feel secure, but it also makes me look inefficient, and it delays getting our business done.	Seek out your boss or a senior coworker right after the next assignment. Tell her or him you're committed to being on time with your work and that you would appreciate her or his feedback along the way so that you can make sure your piece is what the overall project needs. Another alternative might be to collaborate with a coworker whose share of the work is similar to yours.

Here's another example.

Behavior	Triggers	Motivations	Person(s) Affected
Defensiveness	People seem disappointed with something I've done.	I am like a lighthouse, always searching the horizon for potential criticism. I'm afraid the person will be angry with me or, worse still, leave.	My partner
Making excuses	People ask why I did or didn't do something they've asked me to do.	I don't want them to be angry. I don't see why I should take the blame.	My partner, coworkers

In this case, I'm going to remind you of the diet comparison I used earlier. Defensiveness and making excuses are major passive-aggressive traits, so I'm going to ask you to do the *exact opposite* until you are able to find the confident middle ground where assertive personalities live.

Behavior	Assessment of Motivation	New Goals
Defensiveness	The important word here is *seems*. People *seem* disappointed or angry or upset, so I (a) assume that they are and (b) jump in the trenches and get ready to fight.	Be open to taking responsibility. First, make sure that your partner *is* upset. "Have I done something to upset you?" is a good place to begin—but mean it sincerely, and be ready to listen to what you've done. If there is a problem, take responsiblity for it. "How can I make this up to you?" "What can I do to make it better?"
Making excuses	I'm putting all the blame someplace else instead of seeing what my role might be.	Again, I want you to take the exact opposite posture. "I see that I was wrong here. How can I fix this? Think of the neighbor with the cats. Instead of excuses, say, "I didn't realize until I went to your apartment the first time that I'm really very uncomfort-able with (allergic to) cats. I left plenty of food out, but I under-stand they made a mess. I'm sorry."

And finally, let's look at some serious problems of communication—ambiguity and negativity.

Behavior	Triggers	Motivations	Person(s) Affected
Ambiguity	Any situation in which I'm being asked to make a choice or a decision.	I don't know what I want. My decision might make someone unhappy or get me criticized, rejected, or abandoned. Or I may not want to do it when the time comes. I'm afraid of committing and having to be responsible for my choice.	Partner, friends
Negativity	This is the color of my world. I'm being realistic.	If I expect the worst, I won't be disappointed. I don't want to raise my expectations and be hurt when they don't come true.	Everyone I know

Both of these behaviors reflect an attitude toward life, a style of responding. They're probably rooted in childhood experiences when parents didn't allow a genuine freedom of choice. Even if they asked for your thoughts, they didn't really want an answer — or they wanted *their answer*. You would end up waffling until you could see you were getting close to the right answer. Negativity is even more serious. It blights the landscape of your life and leaves you in perpetual darkness. Still, remember, you have the power to change.

Behavior	Assessment of Motivation	New Goals
Ambiguity	Being indecisive may have been a behavior my parents rewarded, but I can see the trouble it is creating in my present relationships, and I take responsibility for it. Also, I understand that a decision *means* commitment. People expect me to be able to say yes or no and stick with it. That's what adults do.	Make it a rule for the near future that you *always* decide. If someone asks you to dinner, test your thoughts and feelings about the invitation and say yes or no. If someone asks your opinion, give it. No hedging. *Maybe* and *I suppose* and all kindred expressions need to be erased from your vocabulary.

Negativity	Negativity is a worldview. It is not realistic. Reality is much more nuanced. Remember there would be no hole if there weren't a doughnut to surround it. The hole has no flavor and offers no nourishment. It has no value. Start to focus on the doughnut.	Rent the movie *Yes Man*, starring Jim Carrey. It's based on a book by British author Danny Wallace. Finding himself in a dark and negative state, the main character decides to say yes to every opportunity for a year. He has some adventures you may not want to repeat, but on the whole the outcome is positive. Give yourself a more modest goal: Say yes to three opportunities every day, and record them in your journal. Also record how they turn out. In the journal—every night, without fail—record five good things that happened to you that day. No "yes, buts" here. Just the doughnut, not the hole.

Envision a New You

Every day as we talk to ourselves in response to the world around us, we shape who we are. If you have grown up in a passive-aggressive pattern, the picture you paint is probably not pretty: You may be describing yourself in ways that make you feel weak or indecisive or lonely.

You are responsible for your life, and you have the power to change who you are and how others see you. Here's a small change. When you're walking down the street or through the office, let your face fall into a gentle smile—not a toothy grin, but a definitively upturned mouth. You could even let your cheeks lift and crinkle your eyes. See how the world around you changes, and record it in your journal. How do people react to you? How do you feel? If people ask why you're smiling, tell them you're feeling good. My bet is that you will.

Now let's go beneath the skin. What kind of person would you like to be? In particular, what kind of partner would you like to be? What characteristics would improve your relationship? Remember, we're not talking about your partner here. How could *you* change in ways that would make your connection with your partner more loving and intimate? You don't have to remain locked in the old patterns. When people diet, they often put up an old photograph taken when they were at their ideal weight. You can do something similar by creating a word picture of the person you would like to be.

If you are stuck in a passive-aggressive approach, it may be hard to see positive traits in yourself, so think of people you admire. They can be famous people or historic figures, but what we know about them is limited. Instead, look at those nearest to you. Here are some examples.

What I admire about my father

- His word is his bond. He never backs out on a commitment he makes, even when I can tell he feels stuck with it.
- He is a good listener. He hears me out before he tells me what his experience has been.
- He doesn't tell me what to do—instead, he helps me to reason it out for myself.

- He is careful about money, and he always spends on others before he takes care of himself.

What I admire about my friend Fay

- She has a great sense of humor, and she pokes fun at herself, not others.
- Once she's made a decision, she doesn't look back and rehash it.
- She's calm and sensible in a crisis, looking for ways to make it better instead of throwing her hands up.
- She protects herself. When she's tired, she stays home and rests. She says no.

Note that some of these characteristics involve the person, and others deal with how the person relates to others.

Exercise: Traits You Admire

1. Think of some people you admire. Write down their names.
2. For each person, write down at least two positive characteristics.
3. Look over your list. Are there common traits among them? Are there themes like honesty or decisiveness or generosity?
4. Now comes the hard part. Write down at least two positive characteristics of your personality. If you're having trouble, you might ask a partner or friend to help. It's an opportunity to see yourself as others see you.
5. Build a character model, listing the positive traits you already have along with those you most admire in others.
6. Look at your list at the beginning of the day, and keep a lookout for opportunities to be this new person.
7. Look at your list at the end of the day, and write in your journal when you have displayed one of these traits. Be positive.

This exercise gives you a target to shoot for, a portrait of the person you want to be—of the person *you will become* as you trade in your passive-aggressive behaviors for traits and modes of being that enrich your life and your relationships.

Remember that passive-aggression is a behavior pattern developed during the course of childhood as a response to your environment. You weren't born passive-aggressive, and you don't have to go on living that way. You may find it useful to revisit your childhood to recover some of the nuggets of your being before the injuries that initiated passive-aggression.

Exercise: Reclaiming Your Essence

1. Use the mindfulness exercises from Key 3 to anchor yourself in the present and focus your mind on the moment.
2. Think back to yourself at the age of 10 or 12. If that was a particularly traumatic time, think of a year when your life was relatively stable, but you were old enough to consider your future.
3. When you daydreamed, what was your role? Were you a pirate? A nurse? A teacher? A fireman? An explorer? Think about the traits associated with those roles.
4. How did your childhood friends relate to you? When you played together, what was your role? Did you come up with the ideas? Lead the action? Follow happily?
5. What were your favorite kinds of play? Reading? Sports? Drawing or playing music?
6. Think of a happy time. Using your novel-writing skills, describe that time in detail. What were you doing? Who were you with? How did you look and feel?
7. Use the answers to come up with an image of your childhood self. Does it hold characteristics that would enhance your relationships today?

Deep inside, there is a strong, good, loving version of you, and keeping that image in your thoughts can help you as you remake your life. Think of your passive-aggressive behavior as a coat or skin that you can shed. Yes, you've been wearing it for a long time, and people have probably become accustomed to seeing you that way. But they will be happily surprised by the fresher, more confident, more open person who lies underneath. So will you.

Want to get a peek at this new person? Drawing from the exercises in this section, you can come up with a word picture of the person you want to be. Take your time. You're reinventing yourself, and that's important work. Adding to its significance is the impact it will have on every phase of your life—physical, emotional, intellectual, professional, personal—and the people you share it with. It's a great adventure, and you're well on your way.

DISABLE THE ENABLER

Molly *was just 25 when she married a successful 40-year-old studio musician named Chris. Their brief courtship was filled with travel and parties and sex, and faces she knew only from celebrity TV shows and websites—dazzling to a young woman who had dreamed of that kind of life.*

Still, she figured they would "settle down" some after marriage, and when she got pregnant, she was delighted. Chris was not. He insisted that they were not ready to become parents and arranged for her to have an abortion. It wasn't something she wanted, but when Chris got angry, she did what she was told. She wondered at times if she had married her father, an authoritarian figure who had disapproved of her marriage.

Over the next two or three years, Molly tried to open the discussion of family and children on a number of occasions. Sometimes Chris yelled. Other times, he just walked away. He and Molly bought a house, but more and more, he decided to go on road trips on his own. He said it would give her time to build their nest and save some money, too. When her credit cards began to go bad—the account was over its maximum, or payment was long overdue—she began to see the truth.

Now Molly acknowledged that they were not ready to start a family. On advice from a financial adviser, they sold the house, moved back into a small apartment, and paid down their bills. Chris stopped coming to the appointments with the adviser after that, and he refused to give Molly control of their finances. Their debt was still increasing, and Molly was pretty sure that some of the money was going to cocaine. She complained to friends and family, but she didn't blame Chris. All creative people tended to be irresponsible, she said. Having walked into this with eyes wide open—well, maybe not wide enough—she would have to live with the man she married.

She tried to be optimistic long after it made sense. "He's got a good recording gig next month," she would tell her mother, "and then we can make a dent in these bills." But as soon as he got paid, Chris would blow the money. Molly went to his friends and her family for help to keep them going, and when they walked away, she found a sales job at a local store so that she could make enough money to pay the rent and put food on the table. Chris pretended not to notice.

It took 12 years before Molly finally had enough and divorced him. Sadly, half of their debt was legally hers, and she spent the next five years paying it off.

Molly was a classic enabler. She avoided conflict because of fears that were rooted in her childhood, so she reinforced the very behavior that she was hoping to be rid of. Because she shielded Chris from the consequences of his actions, he had no incentive to cooperate with her in changing things.

Not all relationships that involve passive-aggressive behavior go this bad, but the partner on the receiving end at the least is always bewildered and at worst may feel driven to the edge of sanity or an emotional breakdown. In this book, we've said a great deal about how passive-aggressive behavior can bring about this result. And in Key 7, we asked the people who bring a passive-aggressive history to their relationships to take responsibility for the damage they cause and to take steps that can bring them and their partners back from the edge of disaster.

While nothing positive can happen *without* the participation of those who are passive-aggressive, this is not the whole story. People who become their long-term partners—friends, family, lovers, employers, or colleagues—usually bring to the table childhood behavior patterns that enable the relationship to fall into a passive-aggressive cycle from which it may never recover. In Key 8, the focus is on the enabling partners.

In the same way that it takes two to tango, it takes two people to support a passive-aggressive relationship. In the tango, the two figures are close together above the waist, and their legs are briefly entangled in the course of the dance, but their feet may be moving in different steps much of the time. Sometimes, it almost looks like they're trying to trip each other. The dancers' eyes are often cast down, and their attention is seemingly on the elaborate footwork. It's a passionate dance, but one that suggests tension more than love. Regardless of gender, the person with passive-aggressive behavior is the lead in this tango, and the partner simply follows.

In this key, we'll look at ways to recognize the signs that you enable the passive-aggression in your relationship. By doing this, you can learn to stop accommodating bad behavior, interact in ways that do not perpetuate the cycle of abuse, and remain receptive to both the other person's authentic expressions of anger and your own. In order to bring the passive-aggressive tango to an end, you will need to change roles and become the lead in your dance partnership. Then you will have to learn some new steps and teach them to your partner, so that your dance can become more loving and collaborative.

The Enabler in a Passive-Aggressive Relationship

Enablers unintentionally perpetuate the passive-aggressive cycle by failing to hold those using passive-aggression accountable for their actions. They keep quiet when they should speak up, excuse outrageous behavior, and bail the other person out of difficult situations under the guise of being "supportive." They say things like, "He's trying to do better" or "if I say anything, she'll just get mad." They are people pleasers who sometimes spend years hoping that, somehow, things will change.

Characteristics of Enablers

You probably don't think of yourself as an enabler. You are just being supportive, understanding, and patient in your dealings with a passive-aggressive partner. Maybe you do let your partner off the hook when he hurts or disappoints you, but you love him, and isn't love about accepting people the way they are? You try to help your partner out when you can, so that his passive-aggressive behavior doesn't get him in too much trouble. Yes, you probably do most of the relationship work, but you're just giving your partner time and space to change. As much as you love him and as much as you're trying to make the connection work, surely one of these days, he will have to shape up. Or so you think.

What you may not see—what this key is here to tell you—is that you are making a world in which your partner's passive-aggressive behavior "works." Why would he change when you're making his behavior risk free? When there is never any price to be paid for chronic lateness, verbal undermining, or all the other classic expressions of hidden anger we've described in this book? Let's examine your "help" from a different perspective.

Fear of Anger and Confrontation

You may see it as keeping the peace, but avoiding confrontation carries a high cost. Afraid of Chris's anger and unwilling to force a confrontation, Molly had an abortion when she became pregnant and remained silent while Chris drove them toward financial ruin because he didn't want the responsibility of a family. In this book, we have seen how anger puts us in touch with important information about our emotions and boundaries that others are violating. Look at this checklist to see if you have enabler characteristics.

* You have trouble standing up to your partner.
* Peace is more important than honesty in your house.
* Your partner can easily manipulate you by using phrases like "You don't want me to . . ." And "You always . . ."

* You back away from talking about your partner's passive-aggressive behavior when he or she gets angry.
* The smallest expressions of approval or gratitude can make you abandon your anger over passive-aggressive behavior.
* You have a hard time saying no.
* You don't confront your partner about passive-aggressive episodes because you want to avoid feeling guilty.

Taking or Transferring the Blame for Your Partner's Misdeeds

One typical attribute of passive-aggressive behavior is the refusal to accept responsibility for one's actions. Someone else—or the world at large—is always to blame. Enabling partners become active collaborators in this behavior by readily agreeing that the problem is someone else's fault. Instead of helping those with a passive-aggressive personality accept responsibility for what they do, enabling partners are all too ready to point the finger in other directions, even at themselves. Perhaps, out of a misguided wish to protect their partners, enablers will be ready to offer explanations and justifications. To Molly, Chris's erratic and irresponsible behavior had to do with his creativity. He was no doubt happy to accept that explanation. See whether you recognize yourself in the following checklist.

* You quickly apologize for things that are not your fault.
* You take the blame for your partner's behavior.
* You blame other people or circumstances on your partner's behalf.
* You have a store of ready excuses and justifications that you can trot out to defend your partner's behavior when someone questions it.
* Your excuses for your partner's behavior sometimes defy credibility.
* You blame yourself for the problems in your relationship caused by your partner's behavior.
* You feel that if you do something (or everything) better, the passive-aggression will somehow stop.

Taking Responsibility for Your Partner's Life

You may just want to help, but by running around after your partner and cleaning up the difficulties they leave behind, you're ensuring that they will never learn to take care of themselves. Some people will take care of work obligations for a neglectful partner or step in to serve the needs of the partner's family, doing what the partner should do. Molly went to others for financial help and finally got a job, when in fact Chris needed to take care of himself and his obligations to their marriage. Yes, there's a nurturing aspect to all of this, but one that's appropriate to infants and children, not to adults who need to make it on their own. Your partners might have had a difficult childhood, but that doesn't mean you should maintain their childlike approach to life. Do these qualities sound familiar?

* You make your partner's needs more important than yours.
* You "fix" your partner's problems while neglecting your own.
* You bail your partner out of situations that he or she should take care of himself.
* You recruit friends to help you clean up your partner's messes.
* You pick up the pieces created by your partner's behavior so neither of you has to deal with the consequences.
* You feel that you have to compensate for the negative actions of your partner's family.

Denying the Facts

You may be simply naive when you accept your partner's explanation or apology, even though you know, based on experience, that nothing will change. More likely, you are so deeply invested in maintaining the relationship that you refuse to see anything that might make it seem tenuous. You may be able to live this charade for a time, but in all likelihood, you are simply refusing to notice the anger that is growing and festering because of the treatment you have chosen to accept. Here's one final checklist.

* You deny your partner's passive-aggression.
* You deny motivations that are obvious to everyone else.

- You have trouble seeing the dark side of your partner's behavior.
- You trust your partner even after he or she has violated that trust.
- You continually leave yourself vulnerable to being hurt by passive-aggression, even when the warning signs are obvious.

Chances are, you have checked more than one box in this list. The same responses may have more than one underlying cause. For example, you may be avoiding confrontation with your partner because you came from a family where such exchanges were frequent, explosive, and even violent. Or you may feel a desperate need to sustain the relationship at any cost. You may take responsibility for your partner's actions out of a misplaced sense of yourself as a caretaker or because you feel guilt about something that happened long ago. Let's look now at how enabling behavior can develop from childhood.

Patterns from Childhood and Enabling Behavior

A variety of childhood patterns may lead to enabling behavior. Of course, the simplest is the most direct: If one or both parents were enablers, then this is the model of adulthood their children were offered. Children may even be raised in a household with an enabler and a person who engages in passive-aggressive behavior. Now they are equipped not only with a model for themselves, but also with a set of characteristics they will seek out in a mate.

There are a number of other components in a household where potential enablers are raised. See which ones sound like your background.

Emotional Neediness

Needy enablers often come from family environments where there was conflict or divorce. Or their parents may have been physically present but emotionally unavailable. Lacking the social confidence and self-esteem that come from secure and stable affection in childhood, they are particularly vulnerable to any threat of abandonment or rejection. They will do whatever it takes to avoid seeing their childhood pain repeated in current relationships.

Some children learn that "being good" means not holding other people accountable. If your parents let you down, you can't call them on it because they get angry. So you excuse and justify their behavior. People raised in this kind of environment are willing to do whatever it takes to keep from being abandoned. When they find themselves in a relationship with someone suffering from passive-aggressiveness, they will engage in classic enabling behavior, because as long as the passive-aggressive partner is dependent on them and interacting with them, they are getting some kind of attention and approval. In their minds, it's better than nothing.

> *Amber is a lesbian who lives with Rose, a highly skilled accountant, in Chicago. Long before she openly acknowledged her sexual orientation, Amber's family and friends had treated her as something of an untouchable. Once her preferences were made known, her family disowned her. Rose is the first live-in partner Amber has had, and she's desperate to maintain the connection.*
>
> *Amber works at a bookstore—she loves the work, but it pays very little. The household's support depends on Rose, who works at a large consulting firm. Rose hates her job and wants to be a writer, but instead of taking concrete steps toward that new goal, she sabotages her employer with passive-aggressive behavior. She's always saying that if she's fired, maybe she'll travel in Europe for a while. She never says whether Amber would be part of that plan or not.*
>
> *Amber makes excuses and jokes about Rose's self-destructive behavior at the office, and she's done some of the work assignments Rose brings home. She's even brought work to Rose's office after Rose has "forgotten" it at home. She responds to Rose's travel talk with extra efforts to make her happy. She craves Rose's approval.*

Childhood Abuse

People who grew up in households where anger was often expressed loudly or violently will often shrink from the merest sniff of conflict as adults. Accustomed to being the object of physical blows and emotional bludgeoning, they are willing to accept the same as adults rather than take up arms themselves. They are appeasers who will do anything to defuse tension and prevent flares of anger, because conflict is intolerable to them. They often wind up becoming the verbal punching bags of their passive-aggressive partners, and in doing so, they allow their partners to insult, criticize, and belittle with impunity.

> *Luis and Carl have been "best friends" for about 10 years. None of the other guys in their social circle understand why Luis will just stand there while Carl hurls verbal insults at him, including racial slurs. Carl, in turn, is passive-aggressive, and in Luis, he's found a perfect target for his hidden anger.*

Little Grown-ups

Some children grow up with parents who seem to expect them to be little adults. Almost as soon as they can walk, they start taking care of the house and their parents. For these kids, love is conditional on performance, leaving them with poor self-esteem and the need to take care of everyone they come in contact with.

The same kind of outcome can happen with overly authoritative or perfectionist parents. The rigid discipline in such households often involves putting the kids to work early and often, but rather than teaching them responsibility, such action tends to show them that they have a purely instrumental role in the lives of others. They are only as well loved as their last good deed. As grown-ups, they become fixers, the folks who pick up the discarded laundry, do the dishes every night, and prepare last-minute dinners for clients their passive-aggressive partner happened to "forget" were coming over.

> *Nora has been happily married to her high school sweetheart for almost 30 years, and her four-times-divorced mother, Connie, has a habit of expressing her hidden anger at Nora's father by acts of potential sabotage to Nora's apparently suc-*

cessful relationship. Connie changes plans with Nora's family at the last minute, phones at midnight with panicked requests for help in choosing birthday gifts, and "accidentally" leaves things at Nora's house, knowing that Nora will drop everything to make the one-hour round-trip drive to return a compact, comb, or address book. Nora would like to stop accommodating her mother, but she can't. Pleasing and caretaking became her pattern long ago, and she is unable to break free of it.

Guilty History

Some enablers grew up in family environments where making someone feel remorse was the primary means of getting what you wanted.

> "Your father and I work so hard so that you can have new toys. Do you think this is something we enjoy?"
> "While you were out playing with your friends, I cleaned up your room and ironed your clothes. I figured you would be too tired to do the work when you came home."

That guilt persists into adulthood, perhaps with Mom and Dad, but it is also a trait that will be attractive to a person who engages in passive-aggressive behavior. When partners try to hold someone displaying passive-aggression accountable, they are met with phrases like, "Look how you made me feel" and "You just don't want me to be happy." These manipulative tactics provoke a rush of guilt, and the enabler lets the behavior slide again. Eventually, the enabler knows that the confrontation will result only in guilty feelings, so he or she says nothing.

The Enabler Gains

Enablers may feel that a passive-aggressive relationship fulfills their personal needs—but over the course of childhood, they developed unhealthy ways to deal with their needs. While you remain in the passive-aggressive cycle, you're not only enabling the passive-aggression in your partner, but you're also fulfilling your own needs in ways that may in fact be limiting your growth and happiness. You might find it useful to return to Keys 2 and 3 with yourself in mind, looking to your past for approaches to life that don't serve your needs as an adult.

> *Lisa was the daughter of a famous Los Angeles business-man and philanthropist. Her father was working and travel-ing all the time, so she got used to his absence. He was the star, and she kept the home fires burning, watching over her mother, her siblings, and even the household staff. She mar-ried a gorgeous professional athlete who drank too much, did cocaine . . . and also happened to be gone all the time during his sport's season.*
>
> *In childhood, this woman had become used to being the support system for a man who was never available. In her marriage, her coke-addicted husband played that role. Nor-mal for her did not include having somebody who could be there for her in a warm, loving way. In fact, when her husband was on a trip, she invited a guest to come stay with her—an-other addict, a girlfriend who was nevertheless a surrogate husband—so that Lisa could continue to be an enabler.*

Certainly, Lisa's enabling behavior was fulfilling her need: She wanted to be indispensable to someone in her life. In the meantime, she wasn't getting any of the normal adult needs for affection, sharing, and support.

I would encourage you to take a close look at your relationship to see if you are acting as the enabler to your passive-aggressive partner. If this is so, you owe it to yourself to ask some hard questions:

- What emotional need am I trying to meet by enabling my part-ner?
- How did I learn to approach my need in this way?
- Does my approach serve a healthy purpose in my life?

- Would I be better off if I could address the underlying need in a way that was healthier for me?
- Would my partner be better off?
- What can I do to meet my own emotional needs in healthy ways?

For example, most people have a need to care for others—either by helping to resolve their problems or nurturing their well-being. However, emotionally healthy people understand that they need to take care of their own needs as well and that a relationship should support both partners. They respect the other partner's right and ability to take care of themselves.

The material in Keys 1 through 4 can help you to evaluate your own emotions, needs, and boundaries. Doing so can lead to understanding about why you enable your partner's passive-aggression. If you learn to disable your enabling patterns, you can build a strong basis for communicating with your partner and helping him or her to escape the destructive cycle of passive-aggression. Enabling your partner's passive-aggression is not meeting your needs but actually *preventing* you from experiencing your own emotions in healthy ways.

The Enabler Loses

Resignation. In the end, you give up. You conclude that there's nothing you can do or say that will change your partner's behavior. You stay because leaving looks like an even worse option.

Resentment. You build up a store of anger. You tell yourself that your partner has "turned you into" an enabler. The anger you refuse to show may find its way out in a passive-aggressive mirror of your partner's behavior.

Once you get to this point, the relationship is doomed. If you think of a relationship as a loving connection between two people, supported by caring acts and open communication, it's *already* over. What you have is something else entirely.

For an enabler, the tipping point can be as thin as a dime. You tolerate and explain and forgive, and suddenly one small act or word totally upsets the apple cart. You go from "It's all right" to "You'll be hearing from my lawyer." If you had spoken up and addressed the problem five years, two years, or one year earlier, you might have had other options. But now the patient can't be saved. You are so filled with resignation and resentment that you would rather tear everything apart than face the role you played in creating the problem.

This doesn't have to be the end result in your relationship. It can be saved, but you have to start now.

How to Change the Dance: Getting Ready

Regardless of how it may seem to you, the person who brings passive-aggression into your relationship has been taking the lead in the tango. You may feel that you are the person taking care of her and tidying up after the messes she leaves, but she is setting the tone. Think about it. She leads, you follow, and her needs rather than yours are being met.

While it's true that your relationship won't change unless she starts taking responsibility for herself, she is unlikely to take the difficult steps involved as long as your enabling behavior gives her no incentive to change. In Key 7, we worked to help the passive-aggressive parties redefine themselves and create new personal goals for how to be. Now, you need to redefine your proper role in the relationship and what you can expect from it.

There are two more steps you need to take to prepare for the hard work of breaking off the destructive tango and learning a new dance that will bring you and your partner closer together.

Educate Yourself and Identify Your Blind Spots

By buying and reading this book, you have taken an important first step. In the eight keys of this book, you have learned how childhood dynamics led you and your partner to the crossroads where you now stand. You've seen how to bring anger and conflict into more appropriate and positive roles in your life. You've also learned new ways to communicate and interact that can help you break the passive-aggressive spell.

By returning to some of the mindfulness exercises in Key 3, you may be able to identify the "blind spots" in your relationship. These are specific types of passive-aggressive behavior that you are consistently denying, excusing, or taking the blame for—areas where you accommodate, rationalize, or overlook what your partner is saying or doing. The fear that prevents you from seeing and dealing directly with this behavior is your blind spot.

Blind spots often reveal themselves in the feelings that your emotions create in your body. When you feel angry with something your partner does but can't understand the reason why, that's an indication that you may have developed a blind spot. Frequently, people with blind spots haven't established clear physical and emotional boundaries for themselves, so they don't know what is permissible for them to feel angry or hurt about. They often think of their thoughts or feelings as "bad." Feelings are not bad. They simply are, and if they are not experienced and released, they will cause problems. This is why identifying your blind spots is essential if you want to move beyond enabling.

Exercise: Identifying Your Blind Spots

1. Using the mindfulness techniques described in Key 3, find a quiet place where you can be alone for 15 or 20 minutes.
2. Let your mind travel over the last day or two of interactions with your partner. Do you feel your body respond as your thoughts touch that encounter? Is there one exchange that stands out in your mind?
3. Examine that exchange more closely, focusing on how you responded. Did you engage in any of the enabling behaviors described in this key?

- Apologize when you had done nothing wrong?
- Back away from a confrontation?
- Provide an unrealistic excuse for the person's behavior?
- Offer to take care of whatever problem the person was experiencing?

4. Sit quietly with this feeling and see what thoughts come up. What other responses might you have made in the situation?
5. Why did you respond as you did?

It would be helpful to repeat this exercise frequently as you begin to explore your own role in the passive-aggressive tango you and your partner are dancing.

Eliminate Unhealthy Attachment

We tend to have positive thoughts about the word *attachment* and what it means in terms of relationships. We think of the normal feelings of liking people, enjoying their company, sharing their concerns, feeling connected to them even when we're separate. All of these are good, positive feelings that can produce healthy outcomes in our relationships. Some kinds of attachment are excessive, however, and unhealthy. They are also common on the enabler side of the passive-aggressive tango.

Emotional dependence on someone else is *not* healthy. In a good relationship, there's a fair degree of interdependence:

- I rely on you for comfort in my down times, and in return, I am there for you.
- I enjoy being with you, but I can also enjoy things when you are not around.
- I want to contribute to your well-being, and I know that you contribute to mine.
- Together, we are something special, but separate, we are still happy and effective human beings.

Please note that most of these statements are two-sided. I give, but I know that you will return the favor. This rarely happens in passive-aggressive relationships, and those that involve an enabler are particularly one sided. Although people who use passive-aggression are also invested in continuing the relationship, enablers are willing to pay almost any price rather than face the possibility of rejection and separation.

This is not healthy. It is normal for people to find ways to have their own needs met; this kind of self-sacrifice is not love.

Preoccupation with the needs and feelings of others is another warning sign. It is normal for partners to share their worries, but except in the most dire of situations, the individuals turn back to their own concerns. If my partner is facing cancer surgery, I may find it hard to concentrate on a work assignment. If my partner is worried about a client's requests, I can listen with compassion and then go back to my own work. If my partner is wondering what to order for dinner, I might offer a suggestion—or I might just chuckle affectionately and move on.

Please note that these responses show *respect* for the partner's ability to meet the challenges of life. My partner probably knows more about what foods are appealing to her, and I know she's competent at her profession and will figure a way out of her current dilemma. With a cancer diagnosis, I understand that she is facing overwhelming decisions and difficult treatments. I want to be as supportive as I can be through *her* crisis, but I know that it is not *mine*.

In an enabler's attachment, the person who relies on passive-aggressive behavior is virtually absorbed into the enabler's consciousness. Every detail of the partner's life becomes the enabler's concern. Enablers will even watch for signs of potential trouble, providing excuses and explanations before there is any problem.

Rescue behavior related to the partner follows naturally. If I am worried about every little thing that happens to my partner, I will rush in—even uninvited—to take charge and provide solutions. In normal relationships, partners ask for each other's advice, but they understand that the individual has to be comfortable with and take responsibility for the decision. Partners may step in to help out—they may even offer—but they don't wade into the individual's life and start living it for them. They have too much respect for their partner, and their partner has earned it.

Develop Healthy Detachment

The word *detachment* is often associated with a Spock-like lack of emotion and a reliance on rationality. Certainly, using our reason is an element of detachment, but that doesn't mean there's no room for emotion. The choice I'm offering is not between unhealthy attachment and no attachment at all. Instead I'm suggesting that there is a middle ground that is healthier for both you and your partner.

The kind of detachment I'm suggesting means that we lovingly disengage ourselves from our partners to the degree that we respect their right—and their ability—to lead their own lives. And then we let them do it. We give them air and space. It means understanding that we can't genuinely solve their problems for them. We can only apply Band-Aids and pain relievers. Even in the closest of relationships, we need to attend to our own responsibilities and let our partners do the same. Always with compassion and love, but without interference.

> *Nobody in the office understands why Judy, the owner of a St. Louis design agency, is so tolerant of Jason, the main contact at their biggest client, a national retailer. As they see it, Jason is impossible: He changes directions at the last minute, refuses to pay for extra work, and is disrespectful and unprofessional in his exchanges with Judy's staff. He makes life difficult for everyone at the agency.*
>
> *Judy tells them he's basically a good guy who is just trying to get the best possible work from everyone. What she doesn't say is that, in college, Jason dated her best friend. When the two broke up, Jason dropped out of college briefly because he was so distraught. He frequently sought out Judy to complain, not realizing that she had urged her friend to*

drop him. To make it up—as she saw it—she filled out the forms that got him back into school and paid the application fees.

The grades he got, however, weren't good enough to get him into law school. He got a business degree, and he's worked his way up through the retailing company, but from what she's heard, he's had a lot of help along the way. Her way of helping is to take the blame for his bad temper and difficult manner. Building a relationship on her desire to help and her misplaced guilt about what happened, she smooths the waters with her staff.

Judy thinks she's helping, but the truth is that Jason is not benefiting from her concern. Instead, he's going forward on a path that is likely to lead to eventual disaster. Sooner or later, Jason has to accept responsibility for his life. Judy is asking her staff to accept behavior they don't deserve because she feels an irrational guilt for what happened to Jason. It was her best friend, after all, who made the decision to stop seeing Jason.

How to Do a Different Dance: Change the Steps

In order to give your relationship a better chance of survival—and survival in a way that enhances the lives of *both* of you—you need to change the dance. Before you attempt this part of the program, make sure you have given enough time to the earlier parts of this chapter: gaining an understanding of your own behavior and how it contributes to the passive-aggressive tango. You will need a strong personal base in order to accomplish the next goals. Don't shortchange your preparation.

Take the Lead

Through the exercise earlier in this chapter, you have identified some of the communication issues that are particular problems in your relationship. This is your "ready" list for further interactions.

You know what's coming, and you can handle it more effectively now. Perhaps the most crucial element in this step is to learn how to respond when you feel yourself becoming upset or angry.

1. Stop the action. Count to 15, and take some cleansing breaths. Don't speak until you are calm, but don't leave the encounter.
2. Returning one passive-aggressive response for another won't move the issue ahead. The same is true of sarcastic or critical remarks.
3. Remember what you've learned about anger and the productive value it can have in your life.
4. If you are still not calm, tell your passive-aggressive partner that you are upset and need time to sort out your feelings.
5. If you have settled yourself, tell your passive-aggressive partner why you are distressed by this exchange.
6. Use "I" statements. If you say, "You're being unreasonable," your partner can deny it. If you say, "I feel that what you're saying puts a lot of demands on me, and this is why," you've taken away that response.

The great challenge in dealing with people who use passive-aggressiveness is to speak to them honestly about their behavior without provoking defensiveness and denial. Most of the time, they really don't understand why you're angry or upset.

To communicate effectively, you need to lower their fears and apprehensions about conflict, and starting an argument won't help. When you first change the dance by taking the lead, you are likely to find a surprised and resistant partner. He or she has been quite comfortable in the passive-aggressive tango and may not understand the change. One option is to initiate a conversation about the change before you implement it. You might say something like this:

> By reading this book, I've come to understand that my behavior has been enabling the passive-aggressive problems in our relationship. I'm taking responsibility for my contribution to our dif-

ficulties. I've grown to understand why I have been responding this way, and I'm going to do my best to stop. Our relationship is important to me. I don't want to walk away, but I want us to be closer than we have been in the past. I think open communication is a good start.

Review Keys 5 and 6 on assertive communication and conflict resolution for some guidelines on how to proceed. By using "I" statements to describe how your partner's behavior affects you, family members, friends, and coworkers, you avoid blaming or shaming. Instead, you give your partner an empowering opportunity to see the impact of his or her actions and move toward change.

Set Limits

In Key 4, we discussed boundaries and limits. Boundaries outline your own comfort zone. Limits tell the other person what your limits are. Understanding that a person's actions are far more important than words, pay attention to how the two may conflict where your partner is concerned. To make progress in your relationship, you need to manage not just his or her denial but your own. You need to set clear guidelines on the kind of treatment you expect from your partner in the future, call him or her out on every violation, and accept no excuses.

Build on Success

People do better when they feel good about themselves than when they feel bad. This is especially true of people who engage in passive-aggressive behavior, because they are exceptionally sensitive to criticism. They may not have experienced much positive reinforcement, and this will be a way to help them make change. Although you need to remind your partner when your limits are crossed, focusing on failure may lead him to lose hope that he can grow or change.

Focusing on success gives your partner hope that a current difficulty can be overcome. Feeling successful develops self-confidence and self-esteem, and these are important characteristics for the person who is trying to grow out of a passive-aggressive history. Make sure you also take note of the occasions when your partner respects your limits or engages in assertive conversations that speak honestly about his feelings.

Acknowledgment is better than *praise*. Acknowledgments create positive feelings, and they support the behavior you want. They are factual statements recognizing a specific accomplishment, task, or success; for example, "I feel very good about the discussion we've just had on our weekend plans. We were both honest, and I think we reached a conclusion we'll both be happy with."

Praise tends to be general, so it doesn't reinforce specific behaviors. It can also sustain a pattern in which the passive-aggressive person is dependent upon the approval of others. Acknowledgment focuses on positive behavior and encourages more of the same; it stimulates self-satisfaction. Praise motivates your partner to act to please you rather than to accomplish something for the sake of feeling competent.

Looking Ahead

The relationship between Molly and Chris ended badly for both of them. Besides sharing the debt, both parties had lost 12 years in which they might have made progress on improving their emotional health. Molly also lost 12 childbearing years and the family she might have started. This was not an inevitable outcome.

If Molly had taken steps to break the passive-aggressive tango of their relationship, two different roads would have been possible. At worst, she would have understood the situation and left sooner, allowing her to make a new start and new relationships. Or better, she and Chris could have worked toward turning the glamorous beginning of their love affair into a stable relationship, with healthy personalities fulfilling their needs and growing together.

Despite the many challenges in your relationship, a good outcome is possible. You have the tools. The fact that you are reading this book suggests that you also have the attitude to make change. Now all you need to do is take the first step.

Afterword

You now have eight keys in hand to help you eliminate passive-aggressiveness from your life and your relationships. Each key opens the door to new insights about your own feelings and new ways of responding to others.

Key 1	*Recognize your anger* and accept it as your friend—the messenger that tells you when your boundaries are crossed or your needs are unmet.
Key 2	*Reconnect your emotions to your thoughts*, distinguishing facts from beliefs formed in childhood that may be limiting you and your relationships.
Key 3	*Listen to your body*, using the technique of mindfulness to stay in touch with your sensations and emotions.
Key 4	*Set healthy boundaries* around your physical and emotional person so that you have a sense of your own identity and command respect for it.
Key 5	*Communicate assertively* to let others know how you feel and what you need and to more fully understand and appreciate the needs and boundaries of significant others.

Key 6	*Reframe conflict*—understanding that, like anger, conflict is a useful tool for resolving differences in ways that create more intimacy.
Key 7	*Interact using mindfulness*, taking responsibility for meeting the challenges of passive-aggressiveness with a mindful approach to others.
Key 8	*Disable the enabler*, identifying the characteristics that lead you to conspire in your partner's passive-aggressive tango so that you can learn another dance.

In thinking about the eight keys, it is tempting to see the path ahead as a succession of doors, rooms you can pass through toward some magical destination. In fact, you'll be moving back and forth among the keys, depending on the situation you face. For example, in the middle of conflict resolution (Key 6), you may need to return to the basic mindfulness exercises in Key 3 to center yourself and get in touch with your feelings, and if the feeling you identify is anger, Key 1 might help.

Let's see how the eight keys might have changed the relationship between Sarah and Tom, whom you met in the introduction to this book. Tom had brought a history of passive-aggressive behavior to their marriage, choosing to avoid conflict rather than confront his concerns about Sarah's increasing involvement with her career. In turn, Sarah had grown frustrated with trying to deal directly with their problems and was adopting passive-aggressive behavior styles. As you'll recall, Sarah returned home, looking forward to a weekend away with her husband, only to find that he had gone over to see a friend. Tom returned late.

Finally, around 11 p.m., Tom strolled in, looking innocent, as if nothing were going on. Sarah spoke honestly about her feelings.

"I was hoping that we could leave this evening for our trip to the mountains," she said. "I've been looking forward to spending some time together."

"Yes, there hasn't been much of that lately," Tom said. Hearing the sarcasm in his own voice, he took some cleansing breaths. "I'm sorry to disappoint you."

Sarah heard the change of tone. "Aren't you disappointed, too?"

This was a difficult question for Tom, because he was afraid the truth would upset Sarah. "Not really," he said. "We can't—I can't afford that fancy resort. I know you make more money but . . ."

Sarah took in his message. "I wanted to do something special for you to make up for all the time I've spent away. And I wanted a quiet place where we could reconnect."

Tom smiled. "It's quiet here."

"We need to talk," she said. "I don't know what you're thinking anymore."

"I thought you were too busy to care."

She shook her head. "Never. It's late now. Let's talk in the morning."

The following day, they engaged in conflict resolution, with a surprising outcome.

Sarah:	*I'm unhappy with the way my life is going. I enjoy working, but this job is taking too much of my time and energy. I wish I didn't need the money.*
Tom:	*It sounds like you might change jobs but you're worried that we can't afford it. I'm working, too. Maybe if we sat down and looked over our expenses, we could figure out a way to get by with less income from you.*
Sarah:	*You're saying you might be willing to reduce our household income? We might have to sell this house.*

Tom:	*When we bought the house, it was supposed to be a step toward having a family. That was one of our goals when we got married. Now we have the house, but it seems to be taking us along a different road.*
Sarah:	*It sounds like you're disappointed that we haven't had kids yet. I've been thinking about that, too. I'm getting older. Maybe it's time to look at our goals.*

Of course, you won't be able to discard your relationship patterns in a single conversation, or even two. Passive-aggression and enabling behavior both have roots deep in childhood. Nevertheless, they can be discarded. Think of them as old shoes. They might look comfortable, but if you've outgrown them, that's not how they'll feel. They'll pinch your toes and force you to walk in ways that strain your whole body. It takes time and dedication to make mindfulness your default plan for living.

Looking Ahead

Mindfulness is a tool with many uses when you are trying to reduce your reliance on passive-aggressive behavior and enabling responses. When you are mindful, you slow down your reactions as you get some distance from the situation. This allows you to explore your true feelings about what's happening instead of getting stuck in a passive-aggressive loop. Besides putting you in touch with your own feelings, mindfulness helps you to listen more effectively to what your partners are telling you.

It's time to toss the old shoes in the back of the closet and develop a new way to move forward in life. This is not a one-step process but a style of behavior that will require daily attention until it becomes second nature. These five steps are the basics, the essential starting point for change:

1. Acknowledge the reality of your passive-aggressive or enabling behaviors as approaches to life rooted in childhood and now part of your nature.
2. Accept responsibility for what you do, think, and feel.
3. Make a list of the people who have been most frequently injured by your passive-aggressive or enabling behavior. If they are no longer part of your life—and if it's not going to cause further harm—write them a note telling them you understand what you did and apologizing for the pain you caused.
4. For the people who are still in your life, own up to your passive-aggressive behavior and invite them to help you eliminate it from your interactions with them.
5. Make a searching and honest inventory of your most prevalent passive-aggressive or enabling behaviors and their warning signs. Write the results in your journal.

Once you have laid this groundwork, here are some habits that can keep you moving forward:

1. Make a habit of focused mindfulness, at least one 15-minute session daily where you can rest in a quiet place alone.
2. During that session, make an inventory, checking events and exchanges of the past 24 hours for the most common of your unwanted behaviors. Record what you find in your journal.
3. Reward yourself for a day during which you have expressed yourself directly.
4. Reward yourself for a day during which you have listened to others with empathy and understood their concerns.
5. If you slip, take an extra mindfulness session to recommit yourself to your goals. Understand that slipping is okay; the failure would be to give up and not recommit.
6. Keep yourself tuned up in terms of hidden anger, unreasonable fears, negative thoughts and beliefs, and boundaries using the exercises in Keys 1 through 4.
7. With your partner, hold a weekly review to identify the week's highs and lows, using compassionate but assertive communica-

tion. Resolve any lingering conflicts. From time to time, hold a recommitment ceremony in which you renew your pledge to combat passive-aggressive and enabling behavior.

Passive-aggressive behavior, particularly in tandem with an enabling partner, is a challenging cycle, but you can break out of its bonds and move toward greater connection and mutual support. This book provides the way, and you can find the will, the courage, and the passion to go forward. Soon you will find encouragement in the rewards of increased feelings of self-worth and enhanced relationships throughout your life, but especially with the partner you have chosen.

I wish you the best—you deserve it.

Index